Banishing Bullying Behavior: Transforming the Culture of Peer Abuse

Banishing Bullying Behavior: Transforming the Culture of Peer Abuse

Second Edition

SuEllen Fried and Blanche Sosland

ROWMAN & LITTLEFIELD EDUCATION
A division of
ROWMAN & LITTLEFIELD PUBLISHERS, INC.
Lanham • New York • Toronto • Plymouth, UK

Published by Rowman & Littlefield Education
A division of Rowman & Littlefield Publishers, Inc.
A wholly owned subsidiary of The Rowman & Littlefield Publishing Group, Inc.
4501 Forbes Boulevard, Suite 200, Lanham, Maryland 20706
http://www.rowmaneducation.com

Estover Road, Plymouth PL6 7PY, United Kingdom

British Library Cataloguing in Publication Information Available

Library of Congress Cataloging-in-Publication Data
Fried, SuEllen.
  Banishing bullying behavior : transforming the culture of peer abuse / SuEllen
Fried and Blanche Sosland—2nd ed.
    p. cm.
  Includes bibliographical references and index.
  ISBN 978-1-61048-432-9 (cloth : alk. paper)—ISBN 978-1-61048-433-6 (pbk. :
alk. paper)—ISBN 978-1-61048-434-3 (electronic)
  1. Bullying in schools—Prevention. 2. School violence—Prevention. 3. School
children—Conduct of life. I. Sosland, Blanche E. (Blanche Eisemann), 1936- II.
Title.
  LB3013.3.F748 2011
  371.5'8—dc23
                                    2011028575

∞™ The paper used in this publication meets the minimum requirements of
American National Standard for Information Sciences—Permanence of Paper for
Printed Library Materials, ANSI/NISO Z39.48-1992.

Printed in the United States of America

Contents

Preface   vii

Acknowledgments   ix

1   Transforming the Culture   1

2   Dimensions and Overview of Bullying   9

3   Back to Bullying Basics   21

4   Getting Specific about Bullying   35

5   Cyberbullying: Unimagined Cruelty   43

6   Bully-Free Summer Camps   51

7   Bullying from Preschool through Adolescence   59

8   Helping Special Needs Students Achieve Success   69

9   The Challenge of Changing the Culture   81

10   Change Agents   93

11   Empowering Students in the Solution   117

12   Ten Burning Questions Posed by Educators   133

13   Parents as Protectors, Partners, and Change Agents   145

14   Letters from Children   161

Appendix   167

References   169

Index   175

About the Authors   185

Foreword

James Garbarino, PhD
Director, Center for the Human Rights of Children
Loyola University Chicago

While there are fewer than one hundred child fatalities each year at school, literally millions of kids suffer from physical and emotional violence in the form of bullying, harassment, stalking, intimidation, humiliation, and fear. Beyond the rare events of gun shots at school are the common events of psychological stabbings—the millions of kids who suffer emotional daggers to their hearts at school. Sticks and stones (and bullets) may break their bones, but words can break their hearts, a phrase coined by SuEllen Fried in her first book, *Bullies & Victims* (1996).

Banishing Bullying Behavior comes at a time when our national consciousness about the nature and consequences of bullying in schools has risen. But it has been a painful raising process. It was not until the outbreak of school shootings in our country during the 1990s that bullying took its rightful place as a serious issue with far-reaching consequences. Research from the FBI and academic social scientists demonstrated the central role of being bullied in the psychology of youth who reached a breaking point and responded with murderous rage. This recognition led to a new generation of research and programmatic action. We learned that far from being the benign inconvenience some portrayed or the character-building "toughening" that others claimed to see, bullying is traumatic and destructive. We learned that adults charged with the responsibility of building positive social environments in schools are responsible for bullying and preventing it. We learned that mobilizing students to set high standards of caring for their fellows is the best way to prevent bullying. We learned that we need not a "war on bullying," but policies and practices that "make peace with kids."

SuEllen Fried and her colleague Blanche Sosland have brought heart and head to bear in this book. They offer a thoughtful analysis, communicate compassion for targets and perpetrators alike, and explore programmatic efforts to make schools more positive places for children and youth. They reach out to educators, parents, support staff, concerned citizens, and kids themselves in this effort, with guidance. Their book focuses on how the social system of the school plays a decisive role in the process of bullying, sexual harassment, and emotional violence in the lives of children and youth. It includes analyses of special themes for parents, teenagers, and professionals. For example, for parents, an important theme is the need to accept the reality that there is bullying, harassment, and emotional violence in today's schools and use this awareness to form an alliance with other concerned parents and approach the school system together, starting with the principal. For kids the message is that they should not have to take on too much themselves; dealing with bullying, sexual harassment, and emotional violence at school is first and foremost an adult responsibility, but one in which kids can play a role. Indeed research shows that the actions of "witnesses" are critical in whether or not bullying flourishes or withers in a school.

For the professional, the message is to avoid the temptation to see bullying as a personal problem and instead to always look for the workings of the school as a social system. This implies strategies for responding that include character education, better feedback from students, and more explicit demonstration of adult caring in the school. The goal is policies and programs that seek to change the culture of the school. As I see it, expecting to replace bullying with nurturance and peace without changing school climate is unrealistic. It is like claiming to be on a diet by going to McDonald's and eating three Big Macs and two apple pies and seeking to balance this out by drinking a Diet Coke. No, programming to deal with bullying is predicated on efforts to create a more peaceful and supportive school. SuEllen Fried and Blanche Sosland have served up a well-balanced "meal" here for those who care for kids and seek to bring peace and justice to the world they inhabit day after day, month after month, year after year during the first two decades of life.

Preface

"It is no sin to attempt and fail, the only sin is to fail to make the attempt."

—SuEllen Fried

Bullying is not static. Over the years, our awareness and our beliefs have gone through many stages. There was a time when we believed that only boys were bullies. There was a time when we believed that bullying was confined to a fist fight or a beating. There was a time when we believed that bullying was a rite of passage for all children.

Today we have given up every one of those beliefs and more are going by the board with each passing day. The impact of technology/cyberbullying has added a whole new dimension to peer abuse. We also address the crucial role of social media. It is imperative for parents to understand this in order to incorporate it in their parenting. Writing this second edition in 2010 and 2011 has been a time of tumultuous, devastating change on so many fronts. We believe that the crises we face today offer enormous opportunities to rethink some of our cherished ideas and to replace them with concepts that will sustain us in this postcatastrophic era.

Our collaboration began out of our mutual concern for two major issues. One is our anguish about the countless number of children who are being tormented and abused by their peers. How can we allow any children to have so much power? Power that will be detrimental to *their* well-being, as well. The other is our unwillingness, as a society, to support the quantity and quality educators that our children deserve. The cultural change to take us from pain, rage, and revenge to empathy, kindness, and healing will require human and financial resources.

We have partnered to bring fresh perspectives to a topic that now enjoys a tremendous amount of interest and concern. If you Google the term "bullying," you will discover an endless list of links. Though the beginning of our book relies heavily on basic information drawn from SuEllen and

Paula Fried's *Bullies, Targets, & Witnesses—Helping Children Break the Pain Chain* (2003), we have used that foundation to take us into the future with new ideas, resources, and concrete strategies. We have added a chapter on bullying in summer camps and created a separate chapter on cyberbullying. In this second edition we have updated current research findings and added important information from the White House Conference on Bullying Prevention.

More and more children with special needs are entering our school system and deserve serious attention as this relates to bullying. More families under financial stress need support and compassion from our society. The time is ripe to create a culture of caring—for children, for families, for humanity.

We are convinced that childhood bullying infects a much broader playing field than the playground. All bullying behaviors must be banished, beginning in early childhood. Left to fester, there will be toxic consequences.

It will take Change Agents—a tipping point of children, educators, parents, prisoners, policy makers, and citizens to create a culture of caring. There will never be a better time to begin the change we envision.

Acknowledgments

Blanche Sosland, my co-author, has been a blessing to work with on this collaboration. Her instincts were always right on target. Her expertise as a former Director of Teacher Education at Park University added an invaluable dimension. Her belief in my work for many years sustains me. The Sosland family, especially David and Abby, were indispensable to our final product.

My husband, Harvey, rose to every occasion of my infinite needs. His "being there for me" was limitless. He is the irreplaceable anchor in my life. Blanche and I drew heavily on the work that Paula Fried, our daughter, had contributed to two previous books on this topic that she co-authored with me. *Bullies, Targets, & Witnesses*, published in 2003 by M. Evans and Co., in particular, was a source of significant content.

Our sons, Jeff and Marc, contributed in many special ways, as did our seven "miracles"—our grandchildren. They provided personal information scattered throughout our book. I am so proud of Elise Stuewe, Samantha Fried, Joe Fried, Jim Fried, Sam Stuewe, and deeply grateful for the special material from Allison Stuewe and Anne Fried. Camille Fried, my daughter-in-law and an extraordinary fifth-grade teacher at Tillman Elementary School in Kirkwood, Missouri, is a resource I turn to, time and time again.

Betty Barker Bashaw, a cherished friend and respected psychiatrist, shared significant research and information. She never failed to find ways to be helpful to me. Mariner Kemper, CEO of UMB Bank, is ensuring that my program will reach as many children as possible. His support for my program is unwavering and unmatched.

My BullySafeUSA Certified Trainers—Dixie Dakos, Mary Fischer, Jan Klein, Lynne Lang, Vicki Price, Kathleen Saucier, and Deborah Trust were crucial consultants. Debbie Johnston is a stellar advocate for bullying prevention. She's a role model for all of us. Andrew Terranova, PhD, tracked my program for many years, through untimely hurricanes in New Orleans and Ft. Myers, Florida. I can never adequately express my appreciation for his professional participation and persistence. Judy Pfannenstiel provided valuable expertise and time to analyze data for my evaluation.

It has been a pleasure to work with Rowman & Littlefield. Tom Koerner's response to our idea for this book was immediate and sustaining. His sound advice served us well as our book evolved. Rita Blitt and Norman Polsky have been champions for kindness. Robert Goodman is my unfailing technology guru.

A group of women friends for thirty years, the "Watering Hole," brings me such joy and research proves that its members are adding years to my life. Molly Laflin and David Waxse continue to send me resource information I would never have discovered.

Members of Reaching Out from Within, an inmate self-help program in thirteen Kansas correctional facilities, continues to be a weekly source of inspiration to me. Ronnie Rhodes deserves to be singled out. Brad Slaughter and Mark Schotte, of Bark Productions, Kansas City, Missouri, produced my training DVD. I am profoundly grateful to them for making this film. Dr. Linda Tinsley, principal of Blue-Jacket Flint Elementary School, Shawnee, Kansas, and Killeen Koontz allowed me to film their wonderful students.

Malcolm Gladwell's book, *The Tipping Point: How Little Things Can Make a Big Difference* (2002), had a profound effect on my search for practical, innovative strategies to bring about social change. James Garbarino brings such humanity to his role as a researcher. I am very grateful for his meaningful Foreword. The men and women who have participated in my Train the Trainer Institutes feed my soul and provided many stories that are the essence of BullySafeUSA.

Had it not been for Irving Sloan, I might never have been a published author. Irv was a legendary teacher at Scarsdale Middle School, Scarsdale, New York, an author, a social justice champion, and a dear friend who died in 2008. I miss him terribly.

SuEllen Fried

ACKNOWLEDGEMENTS

Continuing to share this remarkable journey with SuEllen Fried is so very special and I am more grateful than words can express. She is truly a role model and mentor, teaching and conveying all the values we hold dear, kindness and empathy at the very top of the list.

To Tom Koerner go my sincere thanks for always being there instantly, across the many miles, with answers to our questions. If the answer doesn't come back within a matter of minutes I become concerned that Tom is sick!

My sincere thanks to Lindsey Shauer and Eric Hardy, editorial assistants, for their ready answers to our many questions.

Most of the individuals acknowledged in our first edition of "Banishing Bullying Behavior" continued to make meaningful contributions as I worked on this new edition. My warmest appreciation to Deborah Howard, Marla Kash, Mathew Rudzik, and Carlos R. Martinez of Paradise Computers, who saved my life when my computer failed me.

To Dr. Debbie Sosland Edelman, Alan Edelman, Dr. Jane and Josh Sosland, Abby Sosland and Mark Goodman, Dr. Jeff and Mindy Sosland, Dr. Rachel Pase Sosland and David Sosland heartfelt thanks for your ongoing vigilance and sharing of the newest research in the field of bullying.

And to the next generation, Alex and Jonathan Edelman who shared their experiences as campers and staff members. Their knowledge and insight in the area of summer camping was invaluable to our work in this area. To Sam, Max and Leah Sosland my thanks for helping me understand where your generation is coming from. You are great teachers.

I am most grateful to friends and family from coast to coast and the United Kingdom who shared so much material they found in current publications and personal experiences: Dr. David and Patty Fost, Morton Sosland, Steve Prince, Nancy Mailman, and Debra Rubin.

Special thanks to Julie Anderson of the American Camp Association who put their whole Research Team to work to be certain that we had the most current research available for our new chapter on bullying in summer camps.

I am most grateful to Joel Goldman, Eric Morgenstern and David Svet who have shared their enormous talent and time with us. They have opened up a whole new world for us.

To the very best sister anyone could ask for, Ruth Fost, I am so grateful that we can share both our personal and professional lives in such a meaningful way. My thanks go to Dr. Art Fost for his ongoing willingness to answer my many medical questions as they relate to bullying and so many other topics.

Many thanks to Harvey Fried and David Sosland who are always ready to bail us out when our computers give us fits. I am in awe of how readily you are able to address all our technological challenges. I owe David a huge debt of gratitude for the countless hours he spent editing our manuscript, far beyond our call for help in the area of technology.

To my quintessential husband, Neil, thank you from the bottom of my heart for always being there for me.

Blanche Sosland

1

Transforming the Culture

*"I don't blame those kids for wanting to get back at those guys. It was horrible
the way they were treated—day after day, after day."*

—Maury, a student

DYNAMICS OF BULLYING

After countless years of listening to students talk about abuse from
their peers, reading reports of students who deliberately killed their
classmates or killed themselves, Fried kept wondering what could be
learned from this tragic pattern. Oftentimes, blameless students who
had never bullied the enraged shooters and might have even tried to befriend them became victims. Beloved teachers who sacrificed their lives
trying to protect students took bullets as well. Young men and women
with bright futures turned to suicide as a solution to the bullying they
experienced. There seemed to be no way to make sense of the horrifying
trail of student deaths.

Beyond explanations about children having easy access to guns, the influence of violent media, and the fears of copycat behavior, Fried searched
for a root that would cover the random and the specific. She ultimately
developed a theory that she believes is the dynamic of bullying—the cycle
of pain, rage, and revenge.

The cycle begins when pain is inflicted and anger begins to simmer. Anger is a state of extreme displeasure, a normal emotion and suggests no level
of intensity. There are many ways to control anger, or at least defuse it. But
anger can turn to rage when the intensity reaches a level that is unbridled
and less likely to be checked.

Imagine a young person who is confronted daily with sexual ridicule and
humiliation, with torment and physical abuse, with isolation and ostra-

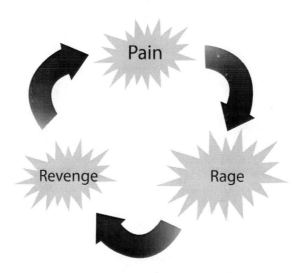

cism from his or her peers. How many adults could survive such a daily onslaught with their dignity intact?

Or a young girl who transmits a nude photo of herself to a trusted boyfriend only to find he has shared it indiscriminately, or a young man betrayed by a roommate who exposes a private intimate act to the multitudes on YouTube. When faced with increasing contempt, an insurmountable balance of power, with no protection by adults in authority, we can understand how pain accumulates and turns to rage or depression.

When enough rage collects, people are consumed with thoughts of retaliation, retribution—revenge. Victims become not only those who were responsible for the actual acts of cruelty, or those who looked on with derision or silence, but those who happen to be in the wrong place at the wrong time. The rage can even take on an entire system.

The violence that erupts causes enormous pain, and the cycle begins again. The pattern often continues into adulthood and escalates into the global conflicts that we are much too familiar with today. Many wars between tribes, countries, regions, and religions can be traced back to pain. With the passage of time, the source of the original pain often becomes lost, even to the combatants—but the vengeance takes on a force of its own.

It is important to remember that the students who brought guns to school and killed classmates and teachers were not the bullies who intimidated their peers. They were the young people, the targets, who absorbed the pain and reached a breaking point where only revenge could satisfy their rage. This statement is not meant to justify their behavior; it is only to underscore the consequence of ignoring their pain.

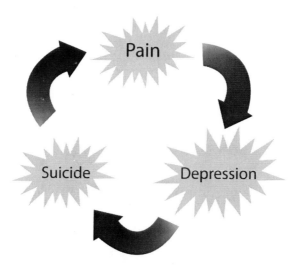

One day, after drawing this cycle of pain, rage, and revenge on a blackboard for a middle-school audience, a student suggested that another cycle might be needed for many children. He said he definitely understood the "pain" part, but it didn't evolve into rage and revenge for him. Aggression was not in his comfort zone. He described how his pain caused him to be depressed and he had considered committing suicide many times. The only factor that prevented him from taking his own life, he confided, was thinking about the pain it would cause for his parents. He suggested the following cycle.

When the pain is turned inward, it can lead to depression. Depression is an indication of repressed anger. The longer it rankles, the more it becomes resistant to a solution. Whether the ultimate consequence is revenge or suicide, the most promising strategy is to prevent pain whenever possible. Even when the pain occurs, there are opportunities for healing. There are ways to deal with it—whether it is expressed overtly or suppressed.

More recently, after drawing both cycles on a blackboard, a middle-school student politely introduced himself at the end of the session and shared that he moves back and forth between these two cycles of pain. Some days he comes to school enraged and plots ways to get back at the students who make his life miserable because he is overweight. Other days, he just feels like giving up and contemplates the easiest way to do away with himself. This confession led to the following illustration.

Some students do both—kill their classmates and turn their guns on themselves. They combine revenge and suicide. Seung-Hui Cho, a student at Virginia Tech, in Blacksburg, Virginia, killed thirty-two people before he took his own life. An effort to find an explanation led to the discovery of a

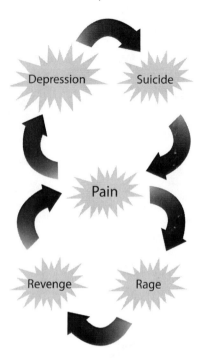

history of peer rejection. There were students and teachers at Virginia Tech who sensed Seung-Hui Cho's loneliness and attempted to reach out to him. It appears, however, that the early rejection and isolation he experienced left him with scars too deep to be assuaged. He transferred his long-held rage to the university, a system that was not the source of his pain.

Such tragedies are all the more reason for us to impress upon young children the need to stop the pain of others whenever possible. It is equally imperative for adults to intervene quickly and consistently when they observe or learn about childhood bullying. Just because students are not acting out in some visible way or screaming at their abusers does not mean they are not suffering. We cannot assume that the absence of expressed distress implies the absence of a problem.

It is important to distinguish between intentional pain directed at us and the universal pain that all of us will experience through loss of a family member; failure of a heavily invested project; rejection by an object of affection; defeat in an election; suffering through a prolonged illness; political, racial, or religious oppression; financial collapse; or various other life experiences. Many have transformed their universal pain into profound life-learning lessons and/or channeled it into virtuous causes for the benefit of others. The universal pain bonds us to every living person and creates an understanding of humanity that transcends all cultures, races, and divisions. That said, we wish to reemphasize that calculated cruelty is unacceptable. It has no place in our schools, playgrounds, buses, summer camps, and social media.

This is an appropriate place to share a lesson learned at a prison in Kansas. It is not about violence, it is about cognitive behavior. Fried is involved in a prison program called Reaching Out from Within, a self-help program for inmates in seven correctional facilities in Kansas. Thirteen groups of men and women meet weekly in various levels of minimum-, medium-, and maximum-security units. At each meeting, one inmate is assigned to facilitate a discussion on a topic such as child abuse, spouse abuse, substance abuse, sexual abuse, anger management, forgiveness, and various other topics that deal with the roots of violence.

One evening Fried attended a meeting at one of the maximum-security units. The topic of the evening was Cognitive Behavior. Ronnie, the inmate chairman of the group, was facilitating the meeting. He began by writing a few words on the blackboard in a prison classroom—attitudes, feelings, behavior. Then he turned to the group and said that he could draw a lot of graphs and charts but he preferred to make the lesson as relevant as possible, and asked if there was anyone in the group that had had a conflict of any kind in the past week.

Rick raised his hand. "Two days ago I got written up for a discipline charge by a guard and I am still furious," he said. Ronnie approached him and asked why he had been written up. Rick replied that another inmate who was a Muslim had an extra prayer rug and gave it to him, even though he, Rick, was not a Muslim. He was happy to have a rug under his feet when he rolled out of his bunk on the cold, concrete floor in the morning. The guard in question stopped by the cell and asked Rick where he got the rug. He made up some story, which the guard later checked out and gave him a write-up for lying.

Ronnie looked at Rick and asked him if he knew that lying to a guard was cause for a write-up. Rick started ranting about the guard and how she always looked for any excuse to write up an inmate and went on and on about the guard.

Ronnie calmly repeated the questions: "Rick, do you know that if you lie to a guard you will get written up?" Rick kept ranting and Ronnie kept repeating the question until Rick finally admitted that he knew the rule. Ronnie then asked Rick, "Why did you lie to the guard?" Rick was clearly upset that he was getting no sympathy for his punishment and in complete exasperation he yelled: "Because the system sucks and the guards suck and I am not going to tell them anything!"

At that point, Ronnie turned to the group, thanked Rick for illustrating the point of the session and stated "Belief trumps reason." "Belief trumps reason" happens more frequently than we realize. If we *believe* that bullying is a childhood pattern of behavior that all children participate in and that if we, adults, just leave things alone, kids will work it out, we are trumping reason. If we *believe* that because we are not observing bullying, it must not be occurring, we are trumping reason. If we *believe* that because something hurtful was truly happening, one of the students would tell us, we are trumping reason.

A sense of relief that abuse isn't happening can turn into a belief. That is why it is so important for adults to be vigilant.

The pain factor in all of deliberations on this theory was most succinctly and purely expressed by a young girl who waited patiently in line at the conclusion of a school assembly to tell Fried something she had learned in Sunday school. "Hurt people, hurt people," she said softly and rushed away to her next class. Her tone of voice revealed that "hurt" was first an adjective and then a verb.

Hurt people, hurt people—so simple, yet so profound. How can we discover these hidden caves of pain inside of our children's souls?

A study by the U.S. Secret Service in the fall of 2000 found that in two-thirds of the thirty-seven school shootings that had occurred since 1974, the attackers felt "persecuted, bullied, threatened, attacked or injured." *Time* magazine, in a May 28, 2001, article, "Voices from the Cell," documented the imprisonment of twelve male teens who killed teachers, students, parents, and/or wounded over fifty others. According to the article by Timothy Roche, "Almost all the shooters were expressing rage, either against a particular person for a particular affront or, more often against a whole cohort of bullying classmates." One of the teen prisoners told a psychiatrist that he felt that going to prison would be better than continuing to endure the bullying at school.

Then there is the case of Andy Williams, the fifteen-year-old student at Santana High School in California, who killed two students and wounded thirteen other people. His classmates had taunted him because of his small size, pale complexion, and high voice. Students would regularly beat him up and call him a "pussy." Following his arrest, Andy told investigators he planned to run away and kill himself after the shooting. Instead, he will spend fifty years in prison—three years in a juvenile prison and forty-seven years in a maximum-security facility. Was there anyone in his school who knew about the bullying? Were there any witnesses who could have intervened in his behalf or alerted adults? Was there anyone who could have changed the outcome for all concerned?

All pain does not turn to revenge or suicide. Some of our most extraordinary leaders and role models have integrated their pain and used it to societal advantage. We must honor those among us who experience pain, from a myriad of sources, and take a different journey. Their path includes reflection, insight, forgiveness, empathy, kindness, healing, and ultimately a passion to reach out to make changes for themselves and others. One person, offering a hand at a poignant moment, can be the transformational figure that moves a targeted child on a different path.

Become a champion for children in pain and you will encourage them to become champions for others and touch the lives of people they will never know.

Mohandas Gandhi and Martin Luther King Jr. are magnificent examples of people who channeled their pain, exorcised their anger, and mobilized legions to bring about unprecedented peaceful, social revolutions.

Many students who are tormented fiercely now will become our teachers, principals, superintendents, and camp directors with the goal to create a caring atmosphere. They will become our counselors, social workers, therapists, and healers. These students will use their pain to find careers and volunteerism that will ease and prevent hurt for those to come.

Our mantra to prevent bullying is directed to the children who are suffering and, in fact, all children suffer when intentional cruelty is permitted to flourish—the targets, the bulliers, and the witnesses. If we can open young people's minds to consider the power of their behavior, if we can open their eyes to the options and possibilities, if we can open their hearts to empathy and kindness and bring about healing, we can make a difference.

The fifth-grade students filed into the room and took their seats. The questions began: "What is physical bullying? What is verbal and emotional bullying?" Robbie knew the answer to all of the questions and gave examples in his soft stuttering voice.

"Why do some students become bulliers?" At first hesitant, then hands flew up. "Because somebody picked on them." "They've got problems at home." "They don't feel good about themselves." "They think it's cool."

"Why do some students become targets?" Lots of students wanted to answer the question. "Because they're different."

The session was coming to a close. "Who can tell me what the word *empathy* means?" queried the speaker. Silence. Then one hand was raised. "It's when you know what someone else is going through," Robbie said wistfully.

"Would all of you please close your eyes? Practice some empathy. Put yourself in the place of someone you know who is having a hard time."

After about a minute, the students were allowed to open their eyes. The last question of the morning was going to be a challenge. "Is there anyone in this room that would like to make an apology to someone you have hurt?" Zachary volunteered to apologize to Robbie. Robbie accepted. Then Brian apologized to Robbie.

"How many students in this room owe Robbie an apology?" Almost every hand went up. "Would all of you please go over to Robbie and let him know that you are ashamed and that all of the bullying is going to stop?" The remorseful students crowded around him and promised they would never taunt him again. Some offered to sit with him at lunch, to play with him at recess.

The teachers and the principal in the back of the room were in tears. As the students left, the teachers told stories of Robbie's isolation. They recalled the day the class played "Red Rover, Red Rover" and Robbie was left standing alone—abandoned by everyone. Today was going to be the day when abandonment would turn to an abundance of kindness for Robbie. The students were empowered and the pain would stop for him.

Eddie had been a student in a mid-size Midwestern, co-ed private school since kindergarten. Jack entered his class in fifth grade. The following year, Eddie started to bully Jack. Whenever Jack did something their classmates thought was "cool," Eddie belittled him in front of his friends. Eddie used an ongoing barrage of verbal bullying.

Jack was afraid to tell his parents because he feared they would do something to make things worse. However, Jack's parents had noted a marked change in his behavior and finally convinced Jack to tell them what was bothering him. They respected his wish not to intervene—until he started vomiting in the middle of the night.

Then they contacted the middle-school principal who in turn met with Eddie and Jack—separately and then together, with Jack's consent. The principal also had a conference with Eddie's parents. She told Eddie that any further bullying was unacceptable and would have serious consequences. She informed Eddie that she would speak to each of their teachers, who would be instructed to report any bullying incidents.

Eddie at this point confided that he was being bullied "big time" by his two older stepbrothers. His parents were completely shocked by this disclosure and took immediate steps to stop the abuse. In a sense, Jack "rescued" Eddie from an intolerable situation.

The bullying did stop and Jack's mom credits the principal for the successful outcome. It took until eighth grade, however, for the boys to become friends. Jack told us that it was "awkward and painful and we didn't become real close until the tenth grade. It was a long healing process."

Jack was willing to share his very painful experience with us because he wants other middle-school students to know what a tough time it is for everyone. He wants them to know that healing is possible—for the bullier and the target. Sometimes it takes a long while—in this case, four years. We can transform a culture of pain, rage, and revenge to empathy, kindness, and healing—youth and adults, parents and educators, all of us together. This is what our book is about.

2

Dimensions and Overview of Bullying

"In the past few years there have been many school shootings.
I think this is due to them kids getting picked on and not let into groups."

—Jeremy, a student

Are there some valuable life lessons that children can learn from bully-ing experiences or is bullying always negative? Is bullying more severe today than it was fifty years ago? Is there a correlation between bullying and other serious social problems? Is bullying a childhood rite of pas-sage or is it a form of child abuse? We will explore these questions in this chapter.

It took SuEllen Fried and her daughter Paula Fried nearly two years to find a publisher for their first book, *Bullies & Victims—Helping Your Child through the Schoolyard Battlefield* in 1996. Bullying was dismissed as a subject without substance or appeal—a childhood rite of passage that is a perennial part of growing up.

However, when radio interviews followed publication, adults flooded the call-in shows. One caller claimed that bullying is an important learn-ing experience about how to defend oneself. Most of the callers, however, recounted painful taunts that linger and sting though many years have passed. Some callers spoke of suicidal thoughts, dysfunctional marriages, the inability to make a commitment to a partner, failed businesses—all directly related to the circumstances of childhood bullying.

The truth is, bullying was horrendous then and it's become lethal now. As we have journeyed into the twenty-first century, seared with tragic images of students fleeing schools, sobbing in each other's arms, and the haunting faces of anguished parents, can we doubt that bullying is excruciatingly dif-ferent from the world of fifty years ago?

Half a century ago it was unthinkable that a child would come to school with a gun and deliberately take the lives of classmates and teachers. School shootings have become a fact of life, and yet too many school administrators have not begun to put comprehensive antibullying plans in place.

The National Youth Violence Prevention Resource Center reports that over 5.7 million students are estimated to be involved in bullying as either a bully, a target of bullying, or both; 13 percent reported that they bullied others, 11 percent were the target of bullying, and 6 percent were both bullies and targets.

A telephone survey, "Talking with Kids about Tough Issues," reported that 74 percent of eight- to eleven-year-olds said teasing and bullying occur at their school, more than the incidence of smoking, drinking, drugs, or sex. The rate increased to 86 percent among children aged twelve to fifteen years old.

The National Education Association estimates that every seven minutes of every school day, a child is the victim of bullying, and 85 percent of the time there is no intervention by other students or adults. Over 280,000 students are physically attacked each month at high schools. One-third of all students say they've heard another student threaten to kill someone. One in five reports they know someone who brought a gun to school. Yet many teachers and school administrators tend to underestimate the problem, which peaks in middle school.

Is bullying an inevitable part of growing up? Does it toughen kids up, teach them how to handle unexpected conflicts and make the transition from childhood to adulthood easier to negotiate? Or is it a traumatic power struggle between youthful, unequal parties—a form of unlabeled child abuse?

Alyssa George, Miss Kansas 2007, a beautiful and bright young woman from a small Kansas community, was a target of bullying during all of her public school years. She was an athlete, a scholar, a talented musician, and extremely attractive. She was painfully ostracized and isolated by her classmates and no matter how hard she tried, was never able to convert their rejection. Her mother repeatedly assured her that the problem was not with Alyssa but with the children who could not handle her many accomplishments. It wasn't until college, when she joined a sorority, that she experienced the novel joy of friendship—a bond that so many take for granted.

All candidates for Miss America were required to choose a platform they would espouse should they be selected. Alyssa chose bullying prevention as her theme and spent a frenetically scheduled year, traveling across the state, making appearances at hundreds of school assemblies, and having a powerful impact on thousands of students. She turned her bullying experience into an amazing calling. She not only touched students' hearts, she affected their behavior with her savvy, engaging style and presentation.

Did bullying "toughen her up?" Did it teach her how to hold on to her self-concept when others were determined to tear it down? Will it prove to be a valuable part of her life? It has often been said that what doesn't destroy us makes us stronger, but we believe that a lesson learned at such emotional expense cannot be justified as tolerance of bullying.

SuEllen Fried and Blanche Sosland, PhD, have been engaged in anti-bullying work for more than fifteen years. Fried has facilitated student empowerment sessions with over seventy thousand students; conducted in-service training for thousands of educators and counselors; and presented seminars to parents and child advocates across the country. Dr. Sosland was a member of the Department of Education at Park University from 1979 to 2000, and served as chairman for a number of years, training thousands of future educators.

Based on their bullying prevention work over these many years, Fried and Sosland maintain that bullying is a form of child abuse—peer abuse. If a child is hurting, it doesn't matter if the perpetrator is a parent or a peer. If a child is suffering, it doesn't matter if the source of the pain is someone who is thirty-five or twelve years of age. No child deserves to be abused—by anyone.

At the conclusion of a professional training workshop conducted a number of years ago, a counselor shared her thoughts. The following is a paraphrase of the conversation:

> In the beginning of this session, when you referred to bullying as a form of child abuse, I reacted negatively and thought you were exaggerating the situation. After being part of this training experience, and listening to the data, I think you should stop using the term "bullying" and use the term "abuse" instead. The term "bullying" is too benign. Too many people associate it with a childhood rite of passage and dismiss its effect. We have to use the strongest language possible to convey what is happening to them and to a number of significant consequences for our educational system.

TRUANCY AND DROP-OUT PROBLEMS

According to the National Education Association, 160,000 children stay home from school every day. They fear what might happen to them on the bus, on the playground, in the cafeteria, in the bathrooms, in the locker room, in the hallways, or in the classroom.

A truancy study looked at twenty-five thousand eighth-grade students in some one thousand schools over time to identify reasons that students drop out of school. Some factors were categorized as "push"—situations from within the school that pushed them out, such as feeling unsafe, feeling like they didn't belong, difficulties with other students, being expelled—while others fell into the "pull" category, external factors that pulled them away from their educational path, such as marriage, pregnancy, having a job, caring for a family member. The push factors appeared to be the most significant for predicting students' decisions to leave school. As a result, one of the suggestions for encouraging students to remain in school was to create a more positive and caring climate. We concur.

Rosemary Menninger, of Topeka, Kansas, shared a recollection of a beloved teacher. "In Mr. Holland's sixth-grade class we participated in a community (our class) that was part of a bigger community (our school and town), part of history, and part of our nation. We felt linked to all of these things, largely through Mr. Holland. We were Mr. Holland's Class, and each of us knew that we were special to him and to each other."

Rosemary went on to describe how Mr. Holland always pointed out special qualities that each student possessed, the strengths of weaker sports players, and the talents of shyer children. He found creative ways to help students deal with prejudices they experienced or prejudices they used against others.

"By October we had begun to gel as a class. Then someone was having a birthday party, and suddenly, the old tradition of inviting only one's favorite friends seemed unthinkable. A new format emerged of inviting the entire class. By Christmas a pattern had been set. Soon, someone in our class would host a party almost every weekend."

Mr. Holland used history, sports, and trivia facts to introduce them to the civil rights struggle of the time, in 1958–1959. His inspiring style of teaching led to Rosemary becoming a teacher and using his techniques to create a sense of family with her students.

LEARNING ISSUES

Students who fear going to the bathroom and freeze at the thought of recess are going to have difficulty focusing on subject matter. Memories of past physical, verbal, emotional, sexual abuse and cyberbullying and terrors about the next assault, interfere with absorbing complicated information. A student consumed with anxiety will have great difficulty concentrating on subject matter.

An example of this situation came to our attention at a private elementary school in Maryland. A parent spoke about her son's sudden drop in grades. Alan, who had always been an A student, was suddenly making Cs and Ds. It took a while to unravel the mystery. The classroom teacher had established a rule that students who had not completed their homework would not be permitted to participate in recess. Bingo! For Alan, who dreaded recess because of the bullying, this rule was his saving grace. He did as much homework as he could during the recess period, but it was never enough to keep him at his previous grade level. Avoiding recess trumped making As for this student.

In light of the No Child Left Behind Act, which focuses on achievement accountability through test scores, a most interesting study has been released. As reported in the *New York Times* (2005), Timothy Shriver and Roger P. Weissberg conducted the largest-ever quantitative analysis, encompassing more than three hundred research studies, to demonstrate the connection between the social and emotional needs of children and their academic performance.

The results show that when children are involved in effective social and emotional learning programs that help them make good choices, avoid bullying, and resist peer pressure to engage in destructive behaviors, they score at least ten percentile points higher on achievement tests than students who do not participate in such programs. The article continues to report that compared with their counterparts outside of these programs, social and emotional learning students have significantly better attendance records; their classroom behavior is more constructive and less often disruptive; they like school more; and they have better grade point averages. They are also less likely to be suspended or otherwise disciplined. This landmark study validates what many professionals have always believed about the connection between bullying and academic achievement.

There is another aspect of academic success and bullying. Some students feel forced to choose between excelling in school and doing poorly to please their peers. Jealousy is frequently mentioned as a cause of bullying.

Jason Potts was unusually bright and overweight. These two factors combined to make Jason a constant target by his middle-school classmates. Jason developed a strategy—lose weight and lower his grades. He stopped raising his hand to answer questions and was succeeding at lowering his test scores. Then he learned about a college prep high school in his urban public-school system that required an application with grade scores for possible acceptance. Jason faced a dilemma. He chose to go for the college prep admission.

Jason graduated from high school with a full scholarship to Yale University. He graduated with a degree in communications and became an assistant producer on *Good Morning, America*. Today he is a TV producer with WCVB-TV, an ABC affiliate in Boston. Years later, Fried commiserated with Potts about the abuse he took as a seventh grader. Jason's reply was: "Don't feel sorry for me. Feel sad for all the kids that gave up their dreams because the peer pressure was too devastating."

We sincerely hope that administrators and educators will recognize that including social and emotional learning will not dilute academic achievement. To the contrary, it offers a strong case to combat truancy, to support academics, and to reduce drop-out rates.

TEACHER SHORTAGES

Richard M. Ingersoll, Professor of Education and Sociology at the University of Pennsylvania, analyzed federal schools and staffing survey data from more than fifty thousand teachers nationwide (2002). Ingersoll reports that 33 percent of teachers leave the field after three years on the job and 43 percent leave within five years.

Suggestions for stemming the tide include increasing support for teachers, raising salaries, curbing student misbehavior, and giving faculty members more say in school decision making. Teachers also expressed concerns about school safety, student motivation, and discipline. Specifically, 25 percent of teachers said that student discipline drove them out and 43 percent left because of inadequate support from school administration.

Teachers today are expected to be educators, social workers, parent surrogates, and law enforcement officers. When we ask students how many of them want to be teachers when they reach adulthood, we are saddened by how few middle- and senior-high-school students raise their hands and are deeply concerned about this consequence for our society.

SUICIDE

In 2010, the Centers for Disease Control and Prevention reported that suicide was the third leading cause of death among youth and young adults in 2007. Though more females attempt suicide than males, males are much more likely to die from suicide. The CDC reports a significant connection between youth who are threatened with or experience physical violence and suicidal thoughts and behavior.

Several studies have shown that gay, lesbian, and bisexual youths face an increased suicide risk. A survey published in the *American Journal of Public Health* (1997) found that gay high-school students were about fourteen times more likely to attempt suicide than heterosexual students.

Many parents have gone public and disclosed the bullying events that led to their children's suicides. Boys who were overweight were taunted, ostracized, and ridiculed beyond endurance. One father spoke of what it was like to cut his son down from the limb of a tree where he had hung himself in their backyard. The boy killed himself because, after a summer of dieting, he looked in the mirror and decided he wasn't thin enough to please his taunting classmates.

The word *bullycide* has now entered our language. Several recent books use this term in their title. Bullycide refers specifically to young people who commit suicide in connection with bullying experiences. One book, *Bullycide in America—Moms Speak Out about the Bullying/Suicide Connection*

(2007), chronicles the suicides of seven students who committed suicide because of bullying. Parents write about the loss of their beloved children because of bullying and document the details that led them to take their own lives. Each heartbreaking story makes us weep. Fried trained one of the mothers, Debby Johnston, who was an eighth-grade science teacher at the time of her son Jeff's suicide. Johnston channeled her anguish into an extraordinary campaign, involving busloads of young people traveling to Tallahassee to persuade the Florida legislature to pass very strong antibullying legislation in 2008.

In 2010, a series of youth suicides occurred within a brief period of time and caused national outrage. The media—TV, radio, newspapers, magazines, and the Internet documented in great detail the individual tragedies and prompted many schools to adopt antibullying policies. Legislators brought the number of states with antibullying legislation to forty-five as of the beginning of 2011. Even the federal government responded with a national summit on the topic.

HEALTH ISSUES

The American Medical Association conducts yearly updates on significant health issues for media sources who write for TV, radio, magazines, journals, and the press. In August 2005, Fried was invited to make a presentation on bullying at such a briefing because of its health implications. Youth suicide is certainly a health issue, but there are others, too. Many mental health professionals report increasing connections between bullying and sleep disorders as well as eating disorder problems for children.

A study conducted at the University of Pittsburgh was the first research in the United States to measure how the hostility level of children affects physical changes such as high blood pressure, body weight, unhealthy blood fats, and "insulin resistance"—ineffective processing of sugar. Karen Matthews tested 134 youngsters ages eight to ten and fifteen to seventeen and followed them for an average of three years. Children who scored at the top 25 percent on the hostility scale were 50 percent at greater risk for type 2 diabetes and heart disease.

There is a vicious cycle at play when children compensate for their lack of successful social relationships by eating comfort foods. Their diet, laden with fats and sugar, causes weight gain and further increases the likelihood of bullying, states Matthews.

The topic of diabetes brings to mind a poignant story conveyed by a mother following a PTA meeting where the subject of peer pressure generated much discussion. She related that her daughter, Mimi, was diabetic and knew that she was not to eat sweets. Whenever her daughter went to a birthday party, in spite of strong parental warnings, Mimi was reluctant to announce that she couldn't eat the birthday cake. In a variety of situations where children were indulging in sweets, Mimi's concern about peer rejection took priority. She felt that refusing cookies, candies, and cakes would make her seem odd.

The mother became tearful and shared that her precious daughter paid a terrible price for her concern about being different and had become blind. Mimi's situation points to the need for education about various health issues that students can understand. Peanut allergies are understood and accepted by children when sound explanations are given. Sugar and gluten abstentions deserve the same presentation.

Though hostility levels are about 30 percent genetic, parents can make a big impact by teaching youngsters how to manage anger and solve disputes without seething inside or erupting. When children observe their mothers and fathers handling competitive drivers and rude behaviors with reasonable responses, they will learn important life skills.

CRIME

More than twenty-five years ago, Leonard Eron, PhD, and his colleagues were one of the first groups of researchers in the country to look at the issue of bullying. Working with a school district in rural upper New York, they invited 875 third-grade students to indicate those classmates they considered to be bullies by putting a check mark beside their name. After collecting the bully nomination forms from the third graders, Eron and his team did extensive interviewing with family members, students, and teachers and stored those files for ten years.

A decade later, when the third graders had become seniors in high school, the researchers repeated the bully nomination process. Not surprisingly, they learned that most of the seniors who were marked as bullies by their peers were the same students identified as bullies when they were in the third grade.

When the original group of students was tracked twenty years later, the research team discovered that one out of every four of the bulliers, tagged by their eight- and nine-year-old peers, had a criminal record by the age of twenty-eight to thirty. The male bullies were at much greater risk of becoming abusive husbands, and the female bulliers were more likely than their counterparts to have become abusive mothers. Other children have about a one-in-twenty chance of becoming adult criminals.

Research indicates that, in addition to criminal behavior, bulliers are more likely to become involved in gangs and/or have employment difficulties, mental health problems, struggles with alcohol and substance abuse, and higher rates of divorce. The children identified as bulliers in the third grade were more likely to become parents of children who were subsequently identified as bulliers by their peers when they were in the third grade. Eron's study was the first to illustrate both the enduring nature of bullying behavior and the apparent intergenerational transmission of bullying behavior.

Support for these findings was demonstrated by Dan Olweus, in a Norwegian study (1993). He found that 60 percent of children identified as bullies between grades six and ten were cited for criminal behavior as adults, and 40 percent had three or more convictions.

Our traditional child-protection system is not set up to protect children from abuse by other children. Adults are protected from assault and harassment and can more readily use the judicial system to charge an attacker. Children, victims of the same assault by a peer, are left to the mercy of adults who may or may not intervene. Child abuse statutes in our fifty states specify the definition of child abuse as maltreatment perpetrated by an adult. Reports of children abused by other children are not customarily investigated by Social Service departments, unless they are sexual in nature.

There are legal aspects of bullying when they become extortion, theft, assault, battery, weapons possession, murder, arson, hate crime, hazing, sexual discrimination, sexual harassment, rape, or a violation of civil rights.

Those reports are handled by the juvenile justice system. Even though this process is quite intimidating, bullying/victim lawsuits are becoming more prevalent. The Howard County school system in Baltimore, Maryland, is facing a ten million dollar lawsuit. The Maryland State Division on Civil Rights, in response to a mother's complaint, determined that the Board of Education had addressed only individual bullying incidents and did not take proactive measures to prevent this behavior school-wide.

In one case, a school district was mandated to pay for the educational and counseling services for two children who had been forced to leave school because of harassment. A school district in Pennsylvania will pay $312,000 to settle a lawsuit filed by a gay teenager who alleged that officials did nothing to stop other students from tormenting him. A jury awarded $250,000 to a Tonganoxie, Kansas, high-school student on the plaintiff's claim that the school district was deliberately indifferent to a same-sex student-on-student harassment in violation of Title IX of the Education Amendment Act of 1972.

A more current issue involves "sexting"—the transmission of sexually explicit photographs by cell phone to each other. In Pennsylvania, three young girls who sent unclothed pictures of themselves to three underage boys who received them were charged by the District Attorney with child pornography. Being charged as a sex offender has lifelong consequences. If any youths are convicted of this felony they will have to reregister as a sex offender wherever they move and their contact with children will be monitored and limited. The repercussions are profoundly serious.

Studies indicate that 20 percent of teens admit to participating in sexting, though sending such pictures is illegal. An Assemblywoman, Pam Lampitt, of Camden, New Jersey, is sponsoring legislation that would give teens an opportunity to avoid prosecution for first-time offenses by completing a diversionary program. Lampitt wants to teach teens the potential consequences of their actions without giving them a permanent criminal record. "We need to create a path that puts education and forgiveness before arrest and prosecution," says Lampitt.

At a meeting of the American Bar Association House of Delegates in February 2011, a resolution was passed that urges federal, state, tribal, territorial, and local officials to prevent and remediate the existence and dangers of bullying, including cyberbullying, and youth-to-youth sexual and physical harassment. The resolution continues with numerous steps to be taken for the prevention and effective intervention of bullying.

SIBLING BULLYING

According to a study published in 2004, more than half of victims of bullying by siblings were also involved in bullying behavior at school compared to only 12.4 percent of those not victimized by siblings, indicating a strong link between intra-familial and extra-familial peer relationships. Children with poor sibling and peer relationships were at a highly increased risk for behavior problems.

The Committee for Children in Seattle, Washington, says a good rule of thumb to determine when sibling rivalry crosses the line to become bullying is: "Behavior that would be unacceptable between two unrelated children is unacceptable between two siblings. When one child intentionally and consistently hurts or frightens a small or less powerful sibling, that's bullying—and it needs to stop."

David Finkelhor, a sociologist at the University of New Hampshire, reported that 35 percent of children had been hit or attacked by a sibling in the previous year (2006). Vernon Wiehe, author and researcher claims that fifty-three out of every one hundred children abuse siblings (1997). Murray Straus, an esteemed sociologist and researcher in the field of family violence, concluded that the sibling relationship was the most violent of human bonds—more than physical abuse of parents to children or husbands to spouses. (1980)

It is not surprising that a boy who was attacked on the school bus by a bullier who forced his neck down between his legs went home and took his rage out on a younger brother by putting him in a stranglehold. Reports from children across the country indicate a strong connection between sibling bullying and peer bullying. Fried and a colleague, Lynne Lang, MHM, have given workshops on this subject at national and international conferences.

When students are asked, "Which troubles you the most—sibling bullying or peer bullying?" many students say that sibling bullying is more hopeless because the "bully" is never going to move away or be expelled. If a parent prefers one sibling over another or if an older sibling is given authority, such as through babysitting, and uses that power to torment freely, with threats of retaliation if the victimized sibling reports the abuse, the abused sibling has no recourse. Concerned responses from students, professionals, and parents are convincing evidence that this issue bears more study and clearly, more action.

Bullying deposits its toxic power in the classroom, the school, the family, the community, the workplace, the nation, and ultimately the world. Educators, counselors, parents, child advocates, business executives, and community activists are the gatekeepers of a civil society and role models for young people who will determine our destiny. There is much work to be done to make the world a kinder place for children.

3

Back to Bullying Basics

"The angel on one shoulder is telling me to do what is right and just.
The devil on the other says just go with the flow or you might be next."

—Clarisse, a student

DEFINING BULLYING

Based on a survey conducted by Fried and Fried, bullying behavior occurs when:
There Is Intent to Harm
The perpetrator finds pleasure in the taunting—physical, verbal, emotional, sexual, cyberbullying—and continues even when the target's distress is obvious.
There Is Intensity and Duration
The taunting continues over a long period of time, and becomes damaging to the self-esteem of the target.
There Is Abuse of Power
The abuser maintains power over his/her target(s) because of age, strength, size, authority, and/or gender.
Bullying behavior is more likely to occur when:
The Target Is Vulnerable
The target is more sensitive to teasing, cannot adequately defend him/herself, and has physical or psychological qualities that make him or her more prone to vulnerability.
The Target Is Unsupported
The target feels isolated and exposed. The target is often afraid to report the abuse for fear of retaliation.
The Target Experiences Significant Consequences

The damage to self-concept is long lasting and the target responds to the abuse with either withdrawal or aggression, which rewards the bullier.

The first three elements focus on the status of the bullier. The last three focus on the status of the target. Because most bullying is unobserved by adults, changes in the behavior of the target might be noticed before the behavior of the bullier is recognized.

EXTENT OF BULLYING

"Bullying Behaviors among U.S. Youth: Prevalence and Association with Psychosocial Adjustment" was published in the *Journal of the American Medical Association* in 2001 and is widely quoted as a major assessment of the extent of bullying in the United States. A representative sample of 15,686 students in grades six through ten in public and private schools throughout the United States completed a self-reporting survey sponsored by the World Health Organization. According to the report, a total of 29.9 percent of the sample reported moderate or frequent involvement in bullying: as a bullier (13.0 percent), one who was bullied (10.6 percent), or both (6.3 percent).

Males were more likely than females to be both perpetrators and targets of bullying. The frequency of bullying was higher among sixth-through eighth-grade students than among ninth-and tenth-grade students. The report extrapolated that 5,736,417 youth are involved in some type of moderate or frequent bullying. The report concludes that "The prevalence of bullying among US youth is substantial" and "the issue of bullying merits serious attention, both for future research and preventive intervention."

It is significant to note that the report did not include data from elementary-school students. We feel strongly that prevention strategies should begin in the primary grades, before students become indoctrinated in the middle-school culture.

A more recent estimate of the extent of bullying comes from Bully Police USA. Based on 2000 census figures and a Norwegian study of Dan Olweus (1997), an internationally respected researcher, there are 8,824,833 students involved as bulliers, targets, and bullier/targets.

BULLYING AS A SOCIETAL CONCERN

The multiple shooting of twelve students and a teacher at Columbine High School by Eric Harris and Dylan Klebold in Littleton, Colorado, on April 20, 1999, was the turning point of the bullying issue in the United States. In addition to the twelve students who died, twenty-three were injured, several critically, and will never fully recover from their injuries.

First reports from the media who interviewed escaping students produced implications that bullying led to the tragic shootings. Once the visual images of students jumping out of windows, children running and crying, armed police officers, sirens, and ambulances became imprinted on the national psyche and was attached to bullying, there was an eruption of interest in the topic. Prior to that tragedy, there were relatively few people who were researching, thinking about, and concerned about bullying. The fact that the Columbine tragedy occurred in an affluent, mostly white suburban school shattered the illusion of immunity from school violence that many had previously held. This combination of factors led to an unprecedented focus on childhood cruelty.

A recent book, *Columbine* (2009), by Dave Cullen, debunks the theory that Harris and Klebold became killers because of bullying. Cullen's thoughtful research indicates that Eric Harris was a brilliant but psychopathic young man who was obsessed with blowing up his high school and found an initially reluctant partner in Dylan Klebold, a depressed fellow student. Though Klebold had known rejection in his school experiences, the carnage he participated in cannot be directly traced to traumatizing bullying at Columbine High School.

Assumptions were made at the time, based on quotes from a very small number of the two thousand students, under inordinate stress. Bullying was a problem at Columbine, as it was and is at schools all over our country, but because of a frenzy to come up with a reason for such a shocking event, those observations became cemented in public opinion.

Twelve years later we have the opportunity to learn new information about what really happened. What cannot be denied is that the cause-and-effect assumptions about bullying led to intense national and international concern. The compelling interest led to tremendous exposure of bullying issues on television, newspapers, radio, and magazines. Surveys, research, programs, and an abundance of materials resulted.

How we wish those students and that teacher had not lost their lives. How we wish the surviving students were not burdened with long-lasting physical and emotional consequences. How we wish the parents of every Columbine student were not scarred by the events of that day. How we wish the principal, administrators, and teachers were not indelibly connected to painful memories. They paid a horrific price for the beginning of our enlightenment about the abuse of bullying. How we wish that years of devoted attention by educators, parents, children, administrators, counselors, medical personnel, mental health professionals, the legal and law enforcement community, foundations, journalists, authors, researchers, theatre groups, filmmakers, songwriters, publishers, government officials, nonprofit agencies, volunteers, survivors, citizens, and legislators had eradicated the problem, but that is not the case.

TERMINOLOGY

Abuse/Bullying

As expressed previously, we will use the terms "abuse" and "bullying" synonymously. An interesting side note is that current reports indicate that 772,000 reports of child abuse are confirmed annually. In response to that appalling data, our society has created multiple resources and responses—including child abuse investigation services, national data collection, foster care and adoption programs, respite care, termination of parental rights, permanency planning, case management, counseling, prevention services, and so on, costing billions of dollars.

For bullying, or peer abuse, which is estimated at between five million and eight million cases annually, there is no national strategy in place. As of this writing forty-five states have passed antibullying legislation, but there are great variations in the bills and many mandates provide no monies or accountability to ensure enforcement of the legislative elements.

Teasing vs. Bullying

Many people believe that teasing and bullying are synonymous, but most students hold to the opinion that all teasing is not bullying. Some teasing is inevitable and can be important preparation for life. Teasing can help us develop a sense of humor, instruct us to be able to laugh at ourselves and teach us to avoid taking ourselves too seriously. We learn how to "take it" and to hold on to who we really are when others attempt to shred our persona. Teasing can also be a way that friends toughen each other up, an adolescent initiation rite. Students define "teasing" when there is mutual give and take, sometimes affectionate—a bantering style of communication where there is equal power.

Bullying, on the other hand, can be described as a situation where one person does all the giving and the other does all the taking. As one bright Kansas student suggested, "Teasing is when two people are laughing, bullying is when only one person is laughing."

Teasing becomes bullying when it ceases to be helpful or playful, when it becomes humiliating and emotionally abusive, and when the target requires protection from the teaser. Should teasing be determined by the teaser or by the person who is being teased? What about those who tease with evil intent, knowing full well that their target is wounded, but claim that "I was only teasing"? Such protests cannot be tolerated as an excuse for cruelty.

Bulliers

There are some who have suggested that we should not label children as "bullies"; that we should talk about children who engage in bullying behaviors lest we stereotype a child who is struggling to find a sense of personal power in a powerless arena. There are some who say that almost every child has been a bullier and/or been bullied and the roles are quite interchangeable. To that point, Dorothy Espelage, PhD, of the University of Illinois at Urbana-Champaign says: "Nearly 80 to 90 percent of adolescents report some form of victimization from a bullier at school, and kids who bully a lot also say they've been victimized." Dr. Espelage believes that we should describe bullying as a continuum of behaviors rather than label any child a bullier, nonbullier, or victim.

A colleague, Lynne Lang, is suggesting that we use the term "bullier" rather than "bully." She feels that referencing the behavior rather than the label is less judgmental.

We concur with those observations. We realize that students move back and forth in the role of targets and bulliers and are often referred to in the literature as bullier/victims. We will be using the term "bullier" as a kind of communication shorthand, and it is very important to us that our readers know our concern is for all children. We believe that every child deserves to be seen as a whole child who behaves in a strategic way toward some end. As one parent pleaded so convincingly: "My child has been involved in bullying behavior on occasion, but if you knew my child, you would never think of him as a bully!"

We recognize that there are some children with severe emotional and mental health problems who lack compassion and empathy, who will not respond to even our most respected interventions and require dramatic courses of action. Such students may require intensive therapy, residential treatment, and removal from their social peer groups.

Targets

SuEllen Fried and her daughter, Paula Fried, used the term "victim" in their first book, *Bullies & Victims—Helping Your Child through the Schoolyard Battlefield* (1996). After working with thousands of students and educators, it became clear that the term "victim" implies helplessness and excludes the power of hopefulness. The Frieds' second book was titled *Bullies, Targets, & Witnesses—Helping Children Break the Pain Chain* (2003).

Thus, we have chosen to use the term "target" because it implies that you may be the object of an attack, but the assault may not be successful. The arrow, so to speak, may completely miss the intended target or, even if it manages to arrive, can be deflected. There are many children who learn how to avoid being victimized by their peers.

WITNESSES

Regarding children who observe bullying, we are committed to the term "witness." Much of the bullying literature uses the term "bystander." This word is too passive and lacks the mobilizing energy that is required of peers to become actively engaged. When asked to define a witness, many students have watched the numerous law programs on TV and are quick to describe a witness as "someone who sees what happens and has to tell the truth." This definition more aptly prescribes one of the actions we heartily endorse for students—to report bullying situations to an adult.

While this may seem to be an obvious reaction, for many children it is fraught with risk. They have concerns about being labeled a "snitch" or "tattletale." In some communities and cultures there is a deeply held code to withhold personal knowledge from authorities. An often-used phrase is, "Snitches get stitches and end up in ditches."

Even teachers who are conscientious about bullying issues don't realize how much abuse occurs when they are not present or aware of the behavior. A study by Wendy Craig from Queen's University and Debra Pepler from York University determined that 71 percent of teachers say they almost always intervene in bullying, while students say that teachers intervene only 25 percent of the time (1997). Pepler and Craig's observations indicate that teachers intervene in 14 percent of classroom episodes and in only 4 percent of playground episodes of bullying.

This discrepancy should not assume that teachers don't care; it is because they aren't there. Bulliers can be Machiavellian in their plots to thwart detection. There are infinite opportunities for students to bully their peers when adults are not around or their backs are turned. The possibilities for abuse on buses and playgrounds and in bathrooms, cafeterias, locker rooms, hallways, and classrooms are infinite.

We are convinced that one of the most hopeful strategies for reducing bullying is to engage witnesses as key players. They are present, they are fully aware of the depth and breadth of the abuse, and they can be provided with skills to use a number of options for prevention and intervention.

Fried attended the sorrowful funeral of a beloved seventeen-year-old student, Bryan Barrow, who died in an automobile accident. At a celebration of his life service, several of his friends spoke about him. One of them, Billy, described an unforgettable moment. He recalled an incident concerning a girl in their class who had no eyebrows. A boy started making fun of her and Bryan said to him, "Why would you say something like that to a girl who is working so hard to stay confident about herself?"

The bullier backed off immediately. Billy was impressed with Bryan's courage and vowed to take similar action when he witnessed an act of cruelty. At the conclusion of the service, everyone was asked to take away one quality of Bryan's to add to their lives as a way of keeping his spirit alive. Hundreds of students left that service with "courage" on their minds and in their hearts. They will be witnesses who make a difference.

ORIGINS OF BULLYING

Family Issues

Bullying is a learned behavior, acquired primarily from family members and/or friends. There is almost universal agreement that bulliers generally become abusers through their life experiences. Bulliers are more likely to have been abused themselves and/or have witnessed their fathers physically abusing their mothers. Bulliers might have been abused by their siblings. When they are unprotected at home, students often use classmates as an outlet for their anger.

Defense Strategy

Many bulliers started out as targets and learned that their best defense was being aggressive. A compelling example came from Mitch, who tried every response possible to avoid fighting back. He tried ignoring the bullier, using his words, reporting the situation to adults, hiding from the bullier, making a joke, but nothing stopped the bullier from tormenting him—day after day after day.

His father kept insisting that the only way to handle such a tyrant was to settle it with his fists. Mitch had no desire to start a fight with Jesse, but after months of relentless bullying, he punched the bullier in the face. To his great surprise, the bullying stopped. Mitch did not want to solve his problem that way. He did not want to become a bullier. But in the end, for him it was the only method that worked.

We include Mitch's story, not because we condone fighting as a defense strategy, but because it reflects a situation we hear much too often. At the same time, it is essential to speak of the risks involved—such as concussions, comas, and a situation in a community in Kansas where two boys became involved in a fist fight and one of them died of a heart attack during the altercation.

Inborn Traits

There are children who are more likely to become bulliers because of inborn traits, such as those who were crack babies, who suffered from fetal alcohol syndrome, and some children with attention deficit disorder (ADD) or attention deficit hyperactivity disorder (ADHD) whose disruptive behavior patterns may have a biological basis.

In the past several years, a mounting number of children who have been diagnosed with Asperger's syndrome, a mild form of autism, are entering the school system. Psychiatrist Leo Kanner was the first person to apply the term "autism" to children who were socially withdrawn, preoccupied with routine, and had difficulty with language yet often possessed a level of intelligence that ruled out mental retardation. The following year, in 1944, Hans Asperger applied the term to children who were socially awkward and consumed with bizarre obsessions, yet highly verbal and very bright. These children have shown up as targets and occasionally bulliers because of social-skill issues.

Media Influence

A large body of research data has confirmed the correlation between TV watching and aggressive behavior. One study followed 707 children in New York for seventeen years. The researchers of the Columbia Country longitudinal study (Huseman et. al.) documented the students' viewing habits beginning in 1983 when they were fourteen years old, and again, eight years later, when they were well into adulthood.

Teens who watched three or more hours of TV a day were five times more likely to commit aggressive acts in the next several years as those who watched less than one hour a day. Among those who watched TV less than one hour a day in 1983, fewer than 6 percent were found to have committed an aggressive act in the next eight years, compared with 22.5 percent of those who watched one to three hours, and 28.8 percent of those who watched more than three hours daily. Acts considered aggressive were assaults resulting in injury, threats of violence, robberies, and use of a weapon in a crime.

Anderson and Dill (2000) have determined that there is an even stronger relationship between playing violent computer games and aggressive behavior. In one study, subjects were asked to play one of two video games: Mist, an analytic virtual computer game or Wolfenstein, a violent video game where the object is to brutally kill their enemies. After playing the video game, subjects were observed in a laboratory with a peer. Subjects who had played Wolfenstein were consistently more aggressive toward the peer.

Other violent video games, such as Grand Theft Auto, have been exposed and deservedly condemned. But then there are those, including our own family members, who point out the value of analytic video games that promote complex thinking and thoughtful responses to solve problems. There are many such games that motivate the player to explore optional solutions to complicated problems. These games, which require work and patience to gather information, stimulate the imagination, and improve skills to create inventive solutions, deserve to be appreciated.

The American Medical Association (2008) contends that media violence causes an increase in mean-spirited, aggressive behavior; causes increased levels of fearfulness, mistrust, and self-protective behavior toward others; contributes to desensitization and callousness to the effects of violence and suffering of others; provides justification for resorting to violence when children think they are right; and fosters a culture in which disrespectful behavior becomes a legitimate way for people to treat each other.

Common Sense Media, a nonpartisan watchdog group, reports that the Kaiser Family study (2010) found that children spend an average of thirty hours a week in school while spending nearly fifty hours a week immersed in media—more than three times the amount of time they spend with their parents.

Profiles of Bulliers

Several researchers have investigated the cognitive process of bulliers. Psychologists Kenneth Dodge, PhD, and John Coie, PhD, (1987) have described two different styles of aggression in their research with children: reactive and proactive.

Reactive bulliers are aggressive children with poor impulse control, and react to an accidental bump as an act of provocation. These children see the world though a paranoid lens, feel constantly threatened, and believe their aggressive response is justified. An accidental brush against their arm can be interpreted as a direct assault. These children do not see themselves as bulliers but as protectors of their space. They see the other child as the troublemaker. These thinking patterns are well in place by the age of seven or eight.

Proactive bulliers, on the other hand, are more calculating about initiating hurtful acts. They behave in a nonemotional, controlled, deliberate manner. They are selective about their targets and look for satisfaction and rewards in their choosing. The aggression is delivered with the hope of achieving some goal that comes from within the aggressive child, like coercion or domination, rather than in response to some external threat.

Robert Selman, PhD, has examined another aspect of the thinking patterns of bulliers (1984). He focuses on the immaturity of bulliers. They lack the more mature form of thinking that allows for a reciprocal exchange of ideas and collaboration that enable people to effectively resolve differences with each other. These bullies have limited skills to manage relationship conflicts and this, in turn, leads to anger and aggression.

The elitist bullier is a third kind of bullier that we have observed. This is the bullier who is very attractive, or is an outstanding athlete, or has acquired social status because of his or her parents' financial, corporate, or political position. Not all children become corrupted by their elitism but a significant number succumb to the power given them and use it to torment those whom they feel are inferior. We have heard countless stories of "jocks," athletes who take advantage of their fame to ridicule and humiliate other students. Often they are even bold enough to do it in the presence of coaches and other faculty members, knowing they will never be admonished. School rules, which all other students are expected to follow, are not applied to them.

A case in point is a young female student, Veronica, at a private school who was extremely malicious and verbally hurtful to students, especially to girls. A classmate commented, "She lives in a palace, she's treated like a princess, and she thinks she is more important than other people." Many mothers consistently complained to the principal, who appeared to be sympathetic to the specific incidents described. However, Veronica's behavior never changed. The parents concluded that because of her family's considerable contributions to the school, the offender would never be reprimanded.

We must observe that many children of high-profile, extremely successful parents are class leaders, are models of considerate behavior, and have learned at an early age to become responsible citizens with a commitment to a greater good.

Profiles of Targets

When students are asked why some of their peers become targets, they usually reply: "Because they are different." However, the list of differences they identify is almost endless—everything from weight and height to hair color and skin color to lack of agility or too much ability. By the time we vet the list, everyone in the class fits into at least one of the categories, so being different cannot be a legitimate reason.

Students become targets because a bullier thinks it's cool to be cruel and gets pleasure out of another person's pain. Some students do seem to send a message that attracts bulliers. It can be in their vulnerable body language, their obvious distress, the way they send some kind of a signal to bulliers on alert.

Gary Ladd, PhD, a psychologist, conducted a study and discovered that bullies engage in a "shopping" process to find students who will become their preferred targets. Ladd suggests that bulliers do not pick on others at random, but use a calculating strategy to narrow their selection. While over half of the students in his study reported being victimized at least once a year, and about 22 percent of the students reported being victimized frequently at the beginning of the school year, by the end of the year only 8 percent of students reported being regularly subjected to a bullier's attacks.

Ladd believes that some targets are more likely to reward their bulliers—tangibly by giving up their lunch money, for example, or intangibly by showing distress and giving the bullier a sense of power. These targets are also less likely to retaliate or cause the bullier to be punished.

We have identified these behaviors as the Cry, Comply, Deny, Fly-Off-the-Handle syndrome.

Cry: Targets who cry make bulliers feel very powerful. While crying may be a natural, legitimate response, postponing tears can be very helpful and is highly recommended.

Comply: Targets who willingly relinquish their homework, their lunch money, their lunch, or the ball they are playing with will find the bullier coming back to them over and over again because they offer no resistance.

Deny: Targets who are easily intimidated and pose no threat of reporting their tormentor are more likely to be selected. Even when asked, some targets will firmly deny the identity of their abuser, out of fear of retaliation.

Fly Off the Handle: Targets can be manipulated by bulliers to explode on cue, just as an adult enters the scene. The target is the one that gets in trouble, which gives the bullier enormous satisfaction and pleasure.

Researchers have identified two types of targets. Olweus describes them as passive (anxious and insecure) and provocative (hot-tempered and restless). Passive targets appear to do nothing to invite the bullier's aggression, and also do not attempt to defend themselves when attacked. They are usually soft-spoken, shy, and lack self-confidence.

Provocative targets create tension by irritating and annoying others and are more likely to fight back when attacked. Provocative targets may have ADHD, Asperger's syndrome, or learning disabilities that prevent them from picking up on social cues other children intuitively understand. They can irritate others without even realizing it.

There are some targets who prefer negative attention to no attention at all. They are so starved for recognition that they tolerate abuse as an affirmation of their existence. However, most targets would choose not to be taunted or excluded and would happily trade places with classmates who manage to escape bullying. Targets need to realize that their "flaw" is not the cause of their torment. We need to help them understand that the problem lies with the bullier, not with them. At the same time, we must assist them to understand how their behavior unwittingly contributes to their vulnerability to bullying.

Profiles of Witnesses

What about those children who witness cruelty and feel helpless to alter the situation? If you can't protect others, can you ensure safety for yourself? What are the lifelong effects of guilt brought about by not speaking up?

Numerous parents have described childhood situations in which they were acutely aware of a classmate's raw wounds and did nothing to intervene. Some have even shared poignant stories of having joined the group assault for self-protection. As they watch their children endure the indignities of others, they are racked by painful memories of their own sins of omission and commission.

Nedra, a soft-spoken conference participant from the Midwest, told the story of attending a rural school where most of the children rode the bus. One little girl became the scapegoat for all the other bus riders, who refused to have any contact with her. This woman reported the only fault this girl possessed was to have lived the farthest away. For that reason alone, other children decided to ostracize her. After a while it became habitual, and no one wanted to be the first to contradict the school-bus culture.

Years later, Nedra became a psychiatric nurse. On her first day of employment at a hospital, a patient approached her. The patient stared at her and said, "Do you remember me?" The nurse immediately recognized the woman as the girl who had been ignored all those early years. The nurse replied, "Yes, I do." The patient looked her directly in the eye and said, "I just want you to see where you are and where I am."

These memories haunt the souls of men and women who participated, sometimes inadvertently, in childhood acts of cruelty. They agonize as they try to reconcile the person they are now with the wounds they caused others in the past. We heard the story of a man who chose not to attend his high-school reunion but sent a videotape instead. In the tape he expressed shame and remorse for the hurtful ways he had treated his classmates when he was young. There is a good chance, however, that the people he hurt so badly did not attend the reunion, either. Adults who live with unresolved pain from their childhood frequently avoid contact with any reminders of their painful past.

Sometimes you cannot make amends, but you can atone. Brandi Guardino, a woman who has become dedicated to bullying prevention, shared the following story on a radio interview. When she was in sixth grade, a girl in her class who was quite large for her age started developing more quickly than the other girls. A popular saying at that time was "Where's the beef?" so the kids started calling her "Beefer." One day a substitute teacher called the roll and when she came to the name of the targeted girl, the students said her name was Beefer, so for the next three days the substitute teacher called the girl Beefer. The target was too embarrassed to ask the teacher to call her by her real name.

To add to her humiliation, every day in gym class a group of girls would grab her towel when she stepped out of the shower. She would cower in the corner to hide her body and cried as she pulled on her wet clothes, only to be ridiculed because of the way her clothing clung to her skin.

Years later, Brandi was working for a psychiatrist and was asked to file the chart of a deceased female patient who had committed suicide. The doctor asked her if she knew the former client. She did not recognize the client's name, but when she reviewed the client's history, she realized that the young woman was Beefer. Brandi is now determined to do whatever she can to prevent this situation from happening to another child. While she did not participate in the devastating activities, she feels deep remorse for not making some effort to support the tormented young girl.

One result is that, as president of the Catawba County Medical Society Alliance in North Carolina, she made bullying prevention a priority project for her group. Fried was asked to conduct the BullySafeUSA Training Institute in the North Carolina community for twenty-two school counselors who will now present that program to thousands of students in their local schools. Sometimes there is nothing you can do to erase the sins of the past, but you can use your energy to shape the future.

Fried observes that witnesses react to the bullying they observe in a variety of ways. Their responses fall into several categories.

Blockers: Withdraw from the action and build a wall around their feelings.
Self-protectors: Focus on how to avoid bullying attacks, at all costs.
Judgers: Become annoyed because targets won't defend themselves.
Voyeurs: Receive some sadistic pleasure out of viewing someone else's anguish.
Accomplices: Directly or indirectly support bulliers and give them power.
Empathizers: Feel concern for the targets but lack confidence to intervene.
Champions: Take some action to relieve the target's pain.

Law enforcement officers struggling with increasing violence in their cities are deeply frustrated by the unwillingness of community members to come forward with information about known perpetrators. This resistance is hampering efforts to keep serial criminals off the streets. A change in attitude in our society is long overdue.

On an encouraging note, administrators are pointing out that students are much more likely to report rumors or threats of violence than they were in years past. Young people are learning that silence hurts and they can save lives when they speak up. A number of tragedies have been averted, but without the headlines that shootings attract.

In our purpose to illuminate the definitions and terminology of bullying behavior and the profiles of bulliers, targets, and witnesses, we feel compelled to restate that first and foremost we are holding all children in our embrace. Our shorthand labels are meant to be helpful in grasping the idiosyncrasies of bullying, not to alienate our concern even for young people who are practicing cruelty.

If bullying is a learned behavior, who taught the bulliers how to inflict pain? Why do some children find pleasure in the torment of others? If they are deeply wounded before we discover them, can we make sure they have access to therapeutic interventions? How can we make sure that every child is protected from the onslaught of brutality, humiliation, and isolation? How can we support them to convert their youthful suffering to become adults who are social healers and advocates for kindness?

As we continue analyzing the seemingly infinite elements of our subject, let us never forget we are discussing the fate of those who were innocents, only a short time ago.

4

Getting Specific about Bullying

"When I see bullying I feel really bad for the person that is being picked on and harassed, but then again, I feel good because it is not me being bullied."

—Mandy, a student

PHYSICAL, VERBAL, EMOTIONAL, SEXUAL, AND CYBERBULLYING TRENDS

Bullying, today, is more complex, more lethal, and considerably different in many ways from bullying in the past. Bullying then was typically synonymous with physical abuse, and even the physical abuse rarely resulted in death. The legendary phrase, "Sticks and stones can break my bones, but words can never hurt me" obscured our willingness to take the verbal assaults that children experienced seriously. Emotional bullying, with its invisible fingerprints, was rarely identified, and sexual bullying, with its elements of sexual curiosity and teen angst, was ever present but not as devastating as it has become today. Cyberbullying, the use of various forms of electronic technology to cause pain, really didn't emerge until the twenty-first century, but has quickly taken its place as a viral form of cruelty.

Even our definition of physical bullying requires expansion. Added to yesterday's choking, kicking, and fisticuffs, which produced bruises, welts, and broken limbs, are today's stabbings, shootings, and pipe bombs, which produce gaping wounds, paralysis, lifelong injuries, and death. This ch will explore these various types of bullying in their current f~ is the result of conversations with over ninety thousan ' private, parochial, urban, rural, and suburban schools try, discussions with tens of thousands of educators and significant research.

35

PHYSICAL BULLYING

Students define physical bullying as: punching, shoving, choking, tripping, poking, stabbing, spitting, beating up, kicking, throwing an object at a target, pushing the target into a locker, taking the target's lunch money, giving someone a black eye, tearing a target's clothes, head butting, shooting, swirleys, stabbing, noogies, nipple twisting, jabbing, throwing a target into the trash can, stepping on someone's toes, urinating on a victim, and wrestling holds. One student even reported being held down while cigarette smoke was blown into her mouth until she vomited.

Girls are more likely to slap, pull hair, scratch, pinch, dig their fingernails into each other, or bite. Boys are more likely to punch, choke, kick, throw objects, and use weapons. Boys have mentioned that girls take advantage of their gender, knowing that they can slap, scratch, or pinch with impunity, as it is considered ungentlemanly for the males to retaliate against a female peer. Physical contact of any kind that is hurtful or harmful is a form of physical abuse. Students find it quite easy to give examples:

"This boy would always come up from behind me and pull on my book bag until I lost my balance. Once he did it while I was walking up the stairs and I fell down six or seven stairs onto the concrete landing. All the other students just walked on by and a lot of them laughed."

"I was standing in line in the cafeteria and the girl behind me suddenly attacked me with a broken mirror she had in her purse. She slashed my shoulder and I was bleeding all over my clothes. I was terrified. They took me to the hospital and my attacker was expelled. To this day, I still don't know why she decided to cut on me."

Cutting brings up the subject of self-mutilation. The act of cutting oneself is also referred to as self-injury or nonsuicidal self-injury. Other forms of self-injury include skin picking, biting, and burning, but cutting is the most frequent form. These acts of self-destruction are much too common among teenage girls. Destructive behavior—whether it comes from others or from within, requires intervention.

Though school violence is decreasing in some communities, we've heard countless stories about bloody beatings, fistfights between girls, and the increased use of weapons. Some disturbing trends include the younger age of offending students, the greater availability of guns, and female involvement in physical aggression. In the last months of 2008 there were two reports of female-on-female violence that made national headlines—one involving a shooting, the other a stabbing.

A growing number have given up baseball bats and are using guns. According to the World Health Organization (1989), "In one year, firearms ed zero children in Japan, 19 in Great Britain, 57 in Germany, 109 in

France, 153 in Canada and 5,285 in the United States." Metal detectors in our schools would have been unthinkable a few decades ago.

Whenever we work with police officers, or peace officers as they are called in some places, they remind us that laws designed to protect adults from physical assault are often invisible with respect to children. How can we watch all the footage of playground battles aired on national TV shows—children ganging up and kicking a contorted classmate, videotapes of youngsters pummeling a helpless student, and not make the connection that this is criminal behavior? How can we criminalize adult victimization and then dismiss it as a "rite of passage" when the victim is a student?

VERBAL BULLYING

Defining verbal abuse also obliges us to broaden our long-held ideas. Today's children are exposed to an unconscionable lack of civility. Curse words that were culturally verboten yesterday are in common usage today.

"Trash talk" is currently accepted as the norm. Models for young people in sports, entertainment, and politics have broken all the boundaries of refined behavior. People who engage in questionable ethics are rewarded with fame, power, and money. No wonder, then, that children imitate our current icons and bring to the playground a kind of social warfare that would not have occurred thirty or forty years ago. Young people who have not developed the maturity to sort out fantasy and reality, short-term and long-term consequences, power and control, are parading in an adult world without the inner character to make good choices.

Verbal bullying can be name-calling, put-downs, threatening, cursing, swearing, yelling, making up stories, gossiping, spreading rumors, talking about someone's mother or another family member, telling "mama" jokes, making fun of a target's physical characteristics, imitating a lisp or a stutter, screaming, being sarcastic, ridiculing, making up a derogatory song, daring someone, whispering about a classmate as he or she approaches. Any use of language to hurt a target would qualify as verbal bullying.

Every child can complete the expression that begins with "Sticks and stones . . ." This sentence has been handed down for at least five generations and it isn't true. In *Bullies & Victims* (1996), Fried asked students to change the phrase to "Sticks and stones can break your bones, but words can break your heart." Students shared that a broken bone can heal in a matter of weeks, perhaps a few months, or sometimes even a year but a broken heart may never heal. Here are two stories reported by students:

"There was this one student who wouldn't ever say my first name, but would always call me 'Jew girl.' Then he would go on to say that 'Your people cause all of the wars.' I'm not even Jewish, but my last name could be!"

"My ears stuck out and all the kids started calling me 'Dumbo.' They never let up. I got so sick of it, I begged and pleaded with my parents to let me have surgery to make my ears smaller. They finally agreed, but I will never forget how miserable I was."

Many students have shared their pain about being called names because of their race, culture, size, height, or a perceived shortcoming of some kind. Frequently, students will talk about how much it hurts to have anyone say something about their mother. There is a collection of "mama" jokes that has traveled all across the country, such as "Your mother is so fat that she has to use the highway for a sidewalk." Some students say it doesn't bother them because they know kids are just repeating jokes, but other students confess that it really gets to them to have anyone say something nasty about their mother, regardless of the origin.

On the subject of rumors, a middle-school girl raised her hand one time to ask about "spreading the truth." When asked to elaborate, she said: "What if you confide a secret to a friend and she betrays you and tells everyone in the class what you told her? Does that count as verbal bullying?" Students will always confirm that betrayal of a secret is a form of verbal bullying.

One student asked: "If the secret of a confession is about being abused, shouldn't you tell a trusted adult?" That was an important difference to make.

EMOTIONAL BULLYING

Emotional bullying includes psychological and nonverbal bullying. It is a type of abuse where there is no physical contact and no words are exchanged.

Nonverbal bullying is pointing, staring, mugging, laughing, rolling your eyes, making faces, sticking out your tongue, writing notes, drawing pictures, flicking people off, and using various hand signs that imply "loser," "crazy," or irreverent and sexual innuendos.

Psychological bullying comes in the form of indirect abuse such as exclusion, isolation, rejection, turning your back on someone who is trying to talk with you, shunning, ostracizing, and ignoring. It may be subtle, or it may be overt. Sometimes these natural schisms form between girls who are becoming more interested in boys and girls who still want to spend most of their time with other girls. Frequently, however, this heartbreaking form of abuse is intentional and without apparent reason. While not exclusive to girls, this type of bullying is inflicted more habitually by female students.

One of the cruelest forms of punishment that humans can inflict on one another is total isolation. It appears that the three places in our society where isolation is most likely to occur are in prisons, playgrounds, and summer camps.

Some examples from students of nonverbal emotional bullying are: "Whenever this boy would see me at school, he would make a fist with one hand and then pound it into his other hand. He never hit me, but I never knew if he would try."

"One day when I was changing clothes in the locker room for gym, I opened my locker and there was a drawing of me taped inside the door. I will never forget it. It showed me naked—with a big head, big arms, big body, big legs, and a very tiny 'you know what.' All my friends were standing around waiting for me to open my locker. When I did, they howled with laughter. These were supposed to be my friends. You don't expect your friends to turn on you like that."

Here are some samples of the psychological emotional bullying: "No one ever invited me to their birthday parties, so when my birthday came along, I sent an invitation to everyone in the class. My mom and I baked cupcakes for everyone and we put their names on with icing. We got gift bags for everyone and we planned some special games. It was going to be the best birthday I ever had. On the day of my party, I waited and waited and waited and no one came."

"I dreaded phys-ed! Whenever it came time to pick teams, I knew that I would be the last one picked because I wasn't good at athletics and nobody wanted to get stuck with me. Then when I would mess up and cause my team to lose the game, everyone would make the Loser sign with their fingers. I tried to get out of gym class whenever I could."

The concept of emotional bullying is the most challenging of the five types to convey because it is the most elusive form of cruelty. As one child advocate, Dorothy Dean, stated, "Emotional abuse is the most difficult type of abuse to define and diagnose. Physical abuse, verbal abuse, and some sexual abuse can be documented and verified. The target, if old enough, can describe what occurred. Emotional abuse, however, is intangible. The wounds are internal but they may be more devastating and crippling than any other form of abuse."

SEXUAL BULLYING

Sexual bullying has always included inappropriate touching and sexual harassment. Today's definition of sexual bullying, however, has to include the use of sexual language directed at students regarding homosexuality that has caused tragic results.

Examples of physical sexual bullying that students have described include touching someone in an inappropriate place, lifting up a girl's skirt or pulling down a boy's pants, pushing a boy and a girl together so their bodies touch, brushing against a person on purpose, grabbing a girl's breasts, pinching someone's butt, pulling a girl's bra strap, kicking a boy in his private parts, hugging or kissing someone when that person doesn't wish to be hugged or kissed.

Students frequently use the term "harassment" without knowing what the term means, but one student gave a very professional answer: "Sexual harassment is unwelcome sexual behavior that makes you feel uncomfortable or unsafe." One boy wanted to distinguish touching *with* consent from touching *without* consent. Our concern would be interpretation of consent, for example: "She said 'no' but she didn't really mean it" and then there is reluctant consent in order to be accepted or gain popularity.

One example that came to our attention was the case of a boy who was stripped down to his underwear in the locker room and then thrown out into the hall as students were going from one class to the next. This was described during a discussion with a large group of middle-school students. When it was mentioned, all the students hooted with laughter except for one boy whose face was contorted in pain. It was obvious who had been "pantsed."

Students have spoken of sexual bullying that is also emotional. This can come in the form of pressuring someone to engage in sexual activity that makes him or her feel uncomfortable. It can be certain hand and finger gestures, or licking lips in a suggestive way. One young girl reported that someone kept thrusting pictures of naked people in her face. It can be whistles or rude noises. Girls have also spoken about being manipulated or used so the male can brag about his sexual conquests to peers. Boys can be pressured by their peers to earn "stud" status. They feel they have to insist on having sex with a girl or pretend that they have to escape being branded as gay.

One boy arranged to have a friend of his hide in his bedroom closet with a video camera where a hole had been drilled. The result was a videotape of himself and his girlfriend having sex, unbeknownst to her, to show to his friends. Unfortunately, this is not an isolated case. More recently, it led to the tragic suicide of a talented Rutgers student whose roommate videotaped him kissing a male companion and distributed the tape widely on the Internet.

Sexual emotional bullying can also be a form of gender discrimination—not allowing someone to do something because the person is male or female, such as team sports. Students mention this with great frequency.

Some girls become very competitive about boys in middle school and high school. A lot of bullying between girls at that age revolves around boys. This territorial aspect of bullying appears to be more common among teenage girls than boys.

Then there is the category of sexual bullying that is verbal. In third or fourth grade, if boys and girls even have a conversation with someone of the opposite sex, kids will sing songs like: "Keith and Kayla sitting in a tree, k-i-s-s-i-n-g." By sixth grade, it's dirty jokes and obscene phone calls. One boy spoke about some awful graffiti in the boys' bathroom. Guys would write on the walls that some girl was a "slut" and then other boys would add really nasty comments about things she supposedly did. He said, "These girls would die if they knew what was being written about them."

Sexual bullying can be calling someone the name of a body part or ridiculing someone because they have developed more quickly or more slowly than his or her peers. Girls have mentioned this on many occasions. They have spoken of being called "cows" or "pancakes." As young people approach puberty and hormonal changes take over, they become extremely sensitive about their bodies. It is a time of confusion, stress, and anxiety. Sexual bullying can be spreading sexual rumors about someone that are untrue but wholly believed because of the salacious interest.

Another facet of verbal sexual bullying is the use of words like "gay," "queer," "faggot," "homo," "lesbo," "tramp," "slut," "whore," "ho," and worse. This kind of language is rampant and pervasive, beginning in elementary schools.

We used to be tentative about mentioning some of these words if they were not forthcoming from the students, but circumstances have changed our reluctance. In many cases of multiple school shootings, the particular form of taunting that pushed boys over the edge was the relentless tagging of being "gay," "homo," a "fag," a "pussy," or some other sexually pejorative term. Sometimes students will try to deny the meanness of the word "gay" by claiming that they were referring to the person as "happy." Our response to that disclaimer is to suggest that if you wish to offer a compliment for their cheerfulness, be sure to use words that can't be interpreted any other way. Dodging the slur is *not* acceptable.

At a workshop conducted for professionals, a therapist who works with sex offenders reported to us that 75 percent of the sex offenders that she had worked with disclosed that they had been bullied about their sexuality when they were in school and felt they had to prove their sexuality to themselves and others.

These are challenging issues to address with students, and we know of teachers and administrators who would prefer to avoid them altogether. The fact that students consistently raise these issues with us, often taking great risks in front of their peers to do so, compels us to match their courage with our own. Too many innocent children pay a price for our unwillingness to confront the sexual behavior that happens in our schools.

Sexting is the most current teen aberration. It combines sexual and cyberbullying. Jessica Logan sent a nude a picture of herself to her boyfriend. When they broke up, he sent Jessica's picture to a group of girls. They disseminated the pictures, even to other school sites, and began posting nasty comments about Jessica, calling her a slut and a whore. Their relentless derision ultimately led to Jessica committing suicide.

CYBERBULLYING

As complex and lethal as the more familiar forms of bullying are, the twenty-first century has brought with it an even more devastating, far-reaching form of bullying, namely cyberbullying. The anonymity and unlimited dissemination of this form of harassment takes cruelty to a level never imagined. Bullying at school now extends to bullying in your home and consequently, there is no relief or sanctuary. Cyberbullying is a special challenge for schools because most of the bullying occurs on home computers, while the devastating effects impact the school environment.

We submit that posing these five types of bullying to students is essential if we want them to grasp the breadth and depth of peer abuse. The information they will divulge and the stories they will share will lay the groundwork for behavior changes that must occur.

Because of recent events involving tragic cyberbullying situations, we are choosing to make this topic a separate chapter, chapter 5.

5

Cyberbullying: Unimagined Cruelty

"I can't get away from it—it follows me everywhere!"

—Kathleen, a student

Let's be clear—the tentacles of cyberbullying go beyond any preconceived definitions of bullying. Phrases like "intent to harm," "abuse of power" can't begin to describe the horror.

Students can experience the pain 24/7. The identity of the cyberbullier can be concealed. Someone who heretofore was practically invisible and would never have the nerve to publicly intimidate a peer can savage a person's reputation on a whim. The visible detachment from the victim encourages a greater level of maliciousness. The number of witnesses to the lies, distortions, and exposure is incalculable. The sense of helplessness is overwhelming.

Joel Haber suggests that "A victim who may never have had the power and is Internet savvy can wreak havoc on another kid because of his or her IT prowess. Kids we may never have suspected as bullies before are those we now have to watch out for in the Internet world. Someone once told me that cyberbullying may become the 'revenge of the computer geeks,' but time will tell if these patterns will take hold. In the Internet world, a child who is really skilled on the computer regardless of their physical stature, popularity, likeability, etc., may hold the power."

Students are experiencing infinite ways in which access to the Internet has produced appalling acts of cruelty. For example, "A student found a way to gain my password and proceeded to send a series of hateful letters to my classmates without my knowing about it. I had no idea why people were so ugly to me. My friends wouldn't speak to me and other kids would curse me out."

DEFINING CYBERBULLYING

Many state antibullying laws include cyberbullying or are in the process of making such a change. According to Kowalski, Limber, and Agatston

(2007), cyberbullying is defined as bullying through e-mail, instant messaging, in a chat room, on a website, or through digital messages or images sent to a cell phone. Their important study indicates that the biggest jump in online activity occurs between sixth and seventh grade, and that young girls are more likely to be online than boys and are more likely to use instant messaging.

Hinduja and Patchin (2011) define cyberbullying "as willful and repeated harm inflicted through the medium of electronic text. Computers with Internet access and cellular phones are the primary ways through which bullying occurs." In their research they found that about half of the victims reported being bullied in some way while in a chat room. In addition to chat rooms and websites, cyberbulliers use text messages; steal passwords; engage in online stalking; post hurtful comments on Myspace, Formspring, Facebook, and ChatRoulette; post videos on YouTube; and manipulate any possible opportunity to use their tech savvy to be cruel.

Parry Afteb, an Internet lawyer, is the Executive Director of WiredSafety, a valuable resource on this topic. WiredSafety.org informs us that 90 percent of middle-school students have had their feelings hurt online, 75 percent have visited a website bashing another student, and 40 percent have had their password(s) stolen and changed by a bullier. Students have their own cyberspace shorthand language, a language that few parents and adults understand. WiredSafety also contends that an incidence of cyberbullying has to have a minor on both sides, or at least have been instigated by a minor against another minor.

WHO IS RESPONSIBLE TO RESPOND TO CYBERBULLYING?

Cyberbullying has raised serious issues for law enforcement, school officials, child protection professionals, parental supervision, and freedom of speech advocates. These issues are being addressed in a variety of ways in different situations and locations. A social dilemma exists that has not been resolved. Many school administrators believe that the school cannot and should not be held responsible for every message that every student sends from their home computer. That is a daunting responsibility for our schools to assume.

On the other hand, many students who are being victimized by cyberbullying are reluctant to share that information with their parents for fear that the computer or cell phone will be taken off limits for them. Most parents are not savvy about the various ways that electronic technology can be used to inflict trauma and don't know how to monitor their children's usage, even if they wanted to. Schools may be the only recourse for some students where consequences can come into play.

TYPES OF CYBERBULLYING

Anonymity: When the bullier is able to keep his or her identity hidden by use of aliases or pseudonyms.

Cyber Stalking: A form of harassment. Targets start to believe that cyber stalking may escalate into live stalking. Usually conducted by e-mail or text messaging.

Denigration: Online "dissing." A bullier can post or send rumors, gossip about a person to damage his or her reputation or disrupt friendships.

Exclusion: Intentionally and cruelly excluding someone from an online group. Occurs frequently when teenagers who don't have cell phones are excluded by those who do.

Flaming: An intense, nasty argument that takes place in a chat room, via instant messaging, or e-mail. Vulgar language is often used and capital letters may be used when writing.

Harassment: Occurs when threatening messages are repeated day and night. Some bulliers post these threatening messages on public forums for all to see the threats. Chat rooms and bulletin boards are often used.

Impersonation, Masquerading, or Posing: To be someone else and sending or posting material to get that person in trouble or danger or to damage that person's reputation or friendships. These are elaborate forms of cyberbullying in which the bullier pretends to be someone else and uses someone else's e-mail or mobile phone.

Outing: The public display or forwarding of personal communication—often involving sexual information—such as text messages, e-mails, or instant messaging. Can cause real psychological damage to people being outed and has led to suicide, and often involves sexual information about the person/people being outed.

Pseudonyms or Aliases: Like a nickname, which is used online to keep the bullier's identity secret.

Trickery: Tricking someone to reveal secret information and then sharing it online.

There are endless examples of these types of cyberbullying, which we have gathered from researchers, students, publications, and, of course, the Internet. For instance, a boy posted a horrific essay about a girl on a website that invited visitors to express hatred about her. Word spread quickly and soon it was the talk of the school. Although the posting had not occurred at school, a school administrator checked out the site after a number of students brought it to his attention. The essay was so cruel and damaging that school officials felt some responsibility to intervene. They met with the girl involved, and then the boy, and both sets of parents.

The boy felt deep remorse when he realized that what had seemed like an impulsive and insignificant act had had such a profound effect on the girl. He contacted the website manager and asked to have the essay removed, but the website manager refused, saying that to do so would be a violation of free speech and would constitute censorship.

SEEKING SOLUTIONS

The very least that schools can do is to hold parent seminars on the topic of cyberbullying. The PTA, PTO, or the school district can bring in experts with the most current knowledge who can answer troubling questions from parents. Schools can make it clear that if they receive evidence of cyberbullying that is abusive to a student, they will take the harshest measures possible.

The school can also engage students in the solution. Involve them in a discussion about what they have read on the topic, what their greatest fears are, and how they can repair harm that has taken place. A student task force could organize a Student Bill of Rights regarding cyberbullying. If students would make a commitment not to pass on stinging, cowardly, devastating comments on the Internet, a lot of pain could be prevented. Students should also be informed that technology is becoming more sophisticated every day and anonymous bullying can be detected and exposed. The Student Empowerment Session is a powerful tool to involve students in the solution as discussed in chapter 11.

States from Rhode Island to Oregon are grappling with cyberbullying language and how much responsibility to place on schools. "The kids are forcing our hands to do something legislatively," said Rhode Island State Senator John Tassoni (2007). However, Steven Brown, Executive Director of the Rhode Island branch of the American Civil Liberties Union said it will be difficult to draft a cyberbullying law that doesn't infringe on free-speech rights.

South Carolina, however, passed a law that requires school districts to define bullying and outline policies and repercussions for the behavior, including cyberbullying. One school district has proposed punishments from warnings up to expulsion. The father of a son who committed suicide because of cyberbullying is advocating for laws that would allow victims and their families to pursue civil penalties. This issue will continue to plague us. Will we be able to convince young people to manage their behavior or will we have to take draconian measures, as officials in some states are doing with sexting, to curb senseless, cruel cyberbullying?

Jan Hoffman wrote an in-depth article, "Bullies Go Digital, Parents Play Catch-up," in the *New York Times* Sunday edition on December 5, 2010, describing the heartbreaking plight of parents in this digital age. She pointed out that "It is difficult enough to support one's child through a siege of schoolyard bullying. But the lawlessness of the Internet, its potential for casual, breathtaking cruelty and its capacity to cloak a bullier's identity all present slippery new challenges to this traditional generation of analog parents."

There is growing consensus that the "generation gap" is no longer an acceptable excuse for parents not to take responsibility to learn what they need to keep up with their children in the area of social media. They are buying their children highly sophisticated mobile phones that are really handheld computers. Therefore, parents must take full responsibility to see that their children of all ages use them appropriately. Unfortunately, many children are getting these at such a young age that they don't have the maturity to fully understand the serious consequences of sexting and other illegal uses of cell phones.

One parent told us recently about a situation her daughter, Ellen, found herself in at a club meeting in the fifth grade. One of her classmates was bored, pulled out her cell phone, pulled up a picture of a nude male that she passed around to several of the girls at the meeting. Ellen was shocked, told her mother about the incident, and her mother reported to us "that it would have done no good to talk to this girl's mother. She wouldn't do anything about it."

The American Academy of Pediatrics (2011) reports that "Pediatricians are now adding another topic to their list of questions for visits with school-aged and adolescent patients: Are you on Facebook? Recognizing the increasing importance of all types of media in their young patients' lives, pediatricians often hear from parents who are concerned about their children's engagement with social media."

Dr. Gwenn O'Keefe (2011), co-author of *The Impact of Social Media Use on Children, Adolescents and Families* states, "For some teens and tweens, social media is the primary way they interact socially, rather than at the mall or a friend's house. A large part of this generation's social and emotional development is occurring while on the Internet and on cell phones. Parents need to understand these technologies so they can relate to their children's online world—and comfortably parent in that world." A highly recommended first step is for parents to have a profile of themselves. This will enable them to "friend" their kids and monitor them online.

In his most recent book *The Checklist Manifesto: How to Get Things Right*, Atul Gawande (2009) makes a compelling case for the use of checklists. The following generally accepted checklist for parents should help them successfully scale the steep learning curve they face closing the technology gap between generations.

Parent Checklist

* Monitor social networks, because the most damaging bullying happens there since the attacks are public. Facebook, Myspace, and Formspring are among the most popular. All sites now let users remove comments from their own profiles, sever friend connections, and block and report abuse. Users can also restrict access to a profile using privacy settings.
* Discuss the serious issue of cyberbullying with your children before it occurs.
* Stress the importance of not giving out personal information such as name, address, phone number, pictures, e-mail address, password.
* Convince your children not to open any messages from people they do not know.
* Urge your children to come to you if they receive any messages that make them feel uncomfortable.
* Get the facts; do not respond emotionally.
* Stress that under no circumstances should they respond to bullying messages online.
* Do not delete bullying messages—save them for evidence.
* Print out offending messages.
* Computer should be in an open, central location.
* Monitor your child/children's computer time.
* Set up a Google alert for your child's name.
* Learn how to report abuses to social networking sites and Internet service providers. Many networks have security officers and try to get items down in less than twenty-four hours. On Facebook, go to "Report/Block This Person" or "Remove from Friends," or go to "Report Page." For Myspace, contact "Myspace" on the bottom of any page, go to "Spam," and then click on "Require approval before comments are posted." Formspring advises users not to answer a mean comment and then it won't be seen by anyone. Report harassment by clicking "Help" on any page, or submit a complaint.
* There are several software programs and online services that can help parents detect and address bullying. SafetyWeb and SocialShield are two of the newer services available for a monthly fee.
* If your child receives threats of harm, contact the police or school resource officer who is a school-based police officer. You will need evidence that may be saved in the web browser or printed out. CyberBullyAlert is available for purchase to help preserve messages.

Joel Haber with Jenna Glatzer provide information on almost twenty websites in their book *Bullyproof Your Child for Life* (2007) for parents to use as resources to deal with cyberbullying. The authors give in-depth descriptions of each website and detailed directions on how to use them.

LEARNING TECHNOLOGY SKILLS WITH YOUR YOUNG CHILD

It would be very helpful for parents of young children to learn technology skills with and from their young children. As soon as your child starts to use the computer (many preschools teach computer skills) ask your child to show you what he or she is learning on a regular basis. If this becomes routine, it should continue as the child gets to more sophisticated levels of online use.

The following test of Internet Technology was developed a few years ago by Scott B. Haber when he was a high-school student. We vetted it with current high-school students and were assured that these were the most common terms—"it's a great list"—but that thousands of new terms can now be found at the Text Lingo website. Taking the following test by filling in the words that these Internet terms refer to will give you a feel for the language of the Internet (Answers can be found at the end of the chapter.):

1. lol
2. btw
3. sos
4. nm
5. w/e
6. jk
7. gtg
8. rofl
9. ttyl
10. nmjc
11. L8r
12. BB
13. kk
14. cya
15. gl
16. brb
17. bbl
18. omg
19. ily
20. pos

Conferences that highlight the crisis of cyberbullying are taking place across the country, even extending to the White House. Efforts to inform schools, parents, students, nonprofit organizations, youth groups, and communities are proliferating. If only we would hear the cries of pain before students shoot each other or themselves. If only they didn't have to resort to such lengths to make their voices heard. If only we could find a way to use the technology creatively in a transformational way. It is used to spread pain, but the positive thing is that it can be used to stop the pain. If only . . .

Answers to Quiz:

1. laugh out loud
2. by the way
3. same old stuff
4. not much
5. whatever
6. just kidding
7. gotta go
8. rolling on the floor laughing
9. talk to you later
10. not much, just chilling
11. later
12. be back much later
13. okay
14. see ya
15. good luck
16. be right back
17. be back later
18. oh my god
19. I love you
20. parent over shoulder

6

Bully-Free Summer Camps

"I tried so hard to make friends and no one wanted to be my friend"

— Bryan, a camper

Summer camping celebrated its 150th anniversary in 2011. The Gunnery Camp was founded by Frederick Gunn and his wife Abigail in 1861. They were the headmasters of the Home School for boys in Washington, Connecticut, and took the whole school on a two-week trip, hiking to their destination, where they set up camp. Camp activities included boating, fishing, and trapping. The program was so successful that they continued it for the next twelve summers.

"I have the conviction that a few weeks in a well-organized summer camp may be of more value educationally than a whole year of formal school work," said Charles Eliot, former president, Harvard University, 1922. Almost a century later many educators and child professionals still agree with this statement.

Over eleven million children, youth, and adults attend more than twelve thousand camps (seven thousand sleep-away and 5,500 day) in the United States each summer. Almost half of these individuals, (5.1 million) attend American Camp Association–accredited camps. ACA accreditation requires the camp to undergo a thorough review of over three hundred standards, from staff qualifications and training to emergency management. Accreditation is voluntary.

The ACA (formerly known as The American Camping Association) celebrated its 100th anniversary in 2010.

Day camps offer programs for kids of all backgrounds, ages two to thirteen. Activities include fishing, swimming, rock climbing, golf, tennis, arts and crafts, theatre, music, dance, field trips, and cook-outs.

Sleep-away camps also offer a broad range of activities. In addition to all of the aforementioned possibilities there are opportunities for horseback riding, canoeing, and archery. Some camps specialize in sports, aeronautics, or computers.

The intensity of being together 24/7 without a family presence can be profound—or painful. The possibilities for emotional and physical growth are enormous, but summer camps, like schools and homes, can also be rife for physical, verbal, emotional, sexual, and even cyberbullying. Campers come with cell phones!

Forty-three states and the District of Columbia have camp licensing requirements to establish standards that ensure the safety and well being of their campers. Efforts are being made in the remaining seven states to require licensing as well. And yet, bullying has also become a serious challenge for well-organized summer camps. To compound the problem, bullying before and after camp has created a year-round bullying situation for some campers.

Through numerous in-depth interviews with campers, past and present; parents of campers who were bullied; camp staff; and the research resources of the ACA we are able to share information that should help to banish bullying behavior from the camp environment and to create bully-free bunks. Summer camps should enrich the lives of all campers. The names of the campers and the camp locations have been changed to protect their privacy. We are most grateful for their willingness to share, in some cases very painful experiences and memories, in order to underscore the need to address the challenge of cruelty at summer camps.

Several former campers now in their fifties found that the scars from their camping experiences still hadn't healed. Barbara told us that when she sat down at the computer to write up her camp bullying experience for us she had tears streaming down her cheeks. After all these years she still found it enormously painful to recall that her parents, believing they were doing what was best for her, did not allow her to come home and leave an intolerable bullying situation. She was twelve that summer and said that the worst bullying took place in the showers because she had not physically matured as much as most of the other girls. The feelings of sexual humiliation and helplessness for a pubescent female have been indelible for Barbara.

Each camp session can be very different. Barbara had positive camping experiences during the two summers at the same camp in Wisconsin prior to the summer she was bullied. The same was true for Keith and Patty. Keith enjoyed his two summers at a camp set in the beautiful Pocono Mountains of Pennsylvania before the summer he was eleven and the family took a trip abroad. The next summer he returned to the same camp and was placed in a bunk of twelve boys who had all been together in a bunk the previous summer. Although they bullied Keith the entire summer with name calling, exclusion, and throwing stones at him as he walked the camp paths, Keith "toughed" it out. One of the camp specialists befriended Keith, spent extra time with him, and met his intellectual needs, making the summer tolerable if not what the camp experience should have been.

Patty's Toothbrush

In Patty's case, she also had spent two enjoyable summers at camp in Maine before she turned twelve. Her friend Beth convinced her to come to her camp in the Berkshires, which was also a positive experience. The following summer Patty decided to return to her former camp in Maine. The bunk with her original bunkmates was full so she was assigned to a bunk that had three open beds. The clique in that bunk did not want any additional campers and they made her life miserable from day one. Bullying took the form of constant exclusion, tampering with her personal belongings, and just being really mean. Her parents told me that the camp had a strong antibullying policy in writing and yet no actions were taken by the administration to deal with the bulliers.

The only intervention was by the head counselor, who tried to teach Patty some coping skills. Patty called home every day asking to come home. Finally, the day her bunkmates took her toothbrush, cleaned the shower floor with it, returned it to the original holder and told Patty what they had done after she brushed her teeth, her parents decided to have her return home. They discovered that there were three empty beds in the bunk because three girls who were bullied the summer before had not returned. The tuition for her camp was close to nine thousand dollars, nonrefundable. It's important to note that Patty's brother had a wonderful summer at the same camp.

In sharp contrast, Gary shared his experience at a camp last summer where he was a junior counselor in a bunk of thirteen boys going into sixth grade. Gary had been a camper in this camp for six summers and had also spent the previous summer as a CIT (counselor-in-training). The camp had a strict policy against bullying, which was consistently enforced.

One week into camp there was a serious bullying situation. The director called each camper in the bunk, individually, to his office and in the presence of the counselors and camp social worker heard every camper's side of the story. At the end of the day the bullier was sent home. This director sent the strong message that is needed to shape the camp culture.

CAMP "HOT SPOTS"

Just as there are well-known "hot spots" where bullying occurs most frequently in schools, the same is true for summer camps. Most bullying takes place during "free time"—when campers are on their way to activities, in the showers and after "lights out" when counselors leave their bunks to spend a few hours socializing with their peers. The obvious solution is increased supervision and counselor training. Requiring counselors to stay in the bunks after "lights out" rather than having some free time of their own has become a very controversial issue for camp administrators. The question of campers' physical and emotional safety versus the need for counselors to have time to socialize in the evening is at stake.

PRE-CAMP PROFESSIONAL DEVELOPMENT

Bullying has become a focus of pre-camp training by many camp administrations. ACA camps are required to address the bullying components of that standard. They also provide a number of professional-development opportunities that address bullying, including the Entry-Level Program Staff Certificate of Added Qualification, Webinar for staff on Bullying Prevention, online course Camp Is for the Camper—Building a Sense of Community, as well as conference/training opportunities.

What camps consider to be even more important is the amount of time and energy spent on building a community at camp and the respect for everyone who shares that community. It is the more positive approach to working with campers and staff that results in a caring community and improved emotional self-regulation behaviors. The campers are empowered to report to staff behavior that is inappropriate and/or disrespectful.

All camps should have a policy clearly stating that bullying behavior is unacceptable and that consequences will be rigorously enforced. The policy should be published in all camp literature, on the camp website, and on the camp application. ACA has noted a trend that camps are strengthening their bullying policies. To help in this process they provide resources on their website: www.acacamps.org/child-health-safety/bullying/articles.

CAMPER TRAINING

Campers should be taught the importance of "reporting" any bullying incident as soon as it occurs. Bullying often escalates if proper intervention does not take place promptly. Counselors should explain the difference between "reporting" and "tattling"—that "reporting" gets campers out of trouble while "tattling" gets campers into trouble.

To start the process of bunkmate bonding, we recommend that a counselor-led discussion be held the first night of camp to establish bunk rules. With a well-planned discussion, a few rules should emerge from the campers to include the concepts of respect, kindness, empathy, and understanding the camp's No Bullying policy. The rules should be posted in the bunks and strictly enforced. The key is to have the rules come from the campers and to have the campers take ownership of their rules.

THE ROLE OF COUNSELORS

Seventy-three percent of camp counselors are between the ages of eighteen and twenty-five and between 50 to 74 percent of staff return to the camp they attended as campers. This gives us a very broad range of maturity and experience among counselors. In Barbara's case, her mother attributed part of the problem to the fact that the eighteen-year-old counselor tried to solve the problem by herself. By the time she sought help from the administration, the situation had escalated out of control.

Counselors can be very helpful in encouraging friendships and helping bunkmates bond. One friendship may decrease the possibility of being bullied by 50 percent.

Counselors should help their campers choose activities in which they can shine, have fun, and make friends who share their passion for any given activity. When campers are involved in exciting, enriching camp activities there is a lot less inclination to bully.

The "chemistry" between the counselor and his or her campers is a significant factor for a healthy, happy summer camping experience.

During our interview with Gary he discussed some of the very delicate issues counselors have to be prepared to handle. He said, "Counselors have to be prepared to deal with homesickness, bulimia, bullying, competition, suicide attempts, romances, and on and on and on. Camp is great for some kids and not for others, certainly not the emotionally fragile. They have to be able to take pranks; even the most popular kids have pranks played on them. Kids just like to joke around."

Pete's "Code"

One counselor told us about his twelve-year-old camper, Pete. Pete was a very popular camper who was prone to anxiety attacks. He didn't want his fellow campers to know about them for fear that they would make fun of him, so Pete and his counselor shared a "code." When he felt an attack coming on, Pete would walk up to his counselor and say he was thirsty. They would quietly leave the activity, take a walk, and talk until the anxiety attack passed.

Many years ago Sosland recalls that she was very homesick her first year at camp. She and her younger sister Ruth's "code" was Sosland walking past Ruth's table in the dining hall after a meal and saying, "Let's meet at the

Lake House," a rustic cabin used for various activities. In this lovely setting at the lake, she was able to work through her homesickness without fear of being bullied by her bunkmates.

There are many factors that are involved in making summer camping an enriching experience. With twelve thousand camps to choose from, parents should be able to find a good match for their child/children. The following checklist is designed to aid in that quest.

Checklist for Parents

- * Camps accreditation and/or licensing
- * Qualification of camp director
- * Camp director's philosophy of summer camping
- * Accessibility of camp director to parents, staff, and campers
- * Willingness of camp director to communicate with you to address your personal camp issues
- * Camps stated antibullying policy
- * Level of camp communication with parents before, during, and after camp session
- * Qualifications of staff at all levels
- * Pre-camp staff training
- * Age and experience of counselors
- * Ratio of counselors and campers

JUSTIN'S "BLANKY"

Eight-year-old Justin was excited about joining his older brother and sister at sleep-away camp in the Ozarks for the first time. His parents tried to persuade him to leave his beloved blanky at home, concerned that it might make him a target for teasing and bullying. But Justin insisted that blanky come with him. "If Linus can carry his blanky, so can I!"

Evidently Justin's perceptive counselor was also concerned that blanky might create problems for Justin and suggested that he keep it under his pillow, where it would be there for him at night and "it would be their secret." When Justin wanted to take blanky to flag raising in the morning, his counselor kindly but firmly refused to allow him to do so.

Justin's counselor and junior counselor created a bunk community of happy eight-year-olds. Justin was elected bunk president and by the time his parents arrived on visiting Sunday one of his bunkmates called out to him, "Justin your blanky fell off your bed. I put it back under your pillow," Justin's parents looked at each other in amazement, thrilled that their son was a happy camper in a happy camp community.

Summer camping has a long, rich history. It is an opportunity for campers to make new friendships—in some cases lifelong friendships—for them to develop independence, leadership abilities, and discover new skills and strengths. Our goal must be to create bully-free bunks and camps so that every camper has the opportunity to be enriched by his or her summer camping experience.

Although we certainly don't live in a bully-free world, the goal for every summer camp—residential or day—should be to banish bullying behavior by transforming the culture of pain, rage, and revenge to one of empathy, kindness, and healing. The camp setting is an excellent opportunity to create an environment of caring, respect, and community, starting with the youngest campers and modeled by administration and staff. Every adult— the kitchen staff, the doctors and nurses, the grounds keepers, the bus drivers—have a crucial role to play.

The co-authors of this book can vouch for the valuable, indelible experiences that summer camps were for us.

7

Bullying from Preschool through Adolescence

"I couldn't believe how children were treating each other in the Center."

—Francis, Director of a Child Care Center

In a stunning statement, Dorothy L. Espelage, PhD (2007), reports that "In the 15 years that I have studied bullying and other forms of youth aggression, the children have gotten younger and younger in their manifestations of these behaviors. The behaviors we saw in 5th-graders, we are now seeing in preschool playgroups. I think this is due in part to the introduction of technology to youth and their level of sophistication associated with their targeting each other." This is certainly an urgent wake-up call to address the serious problem of bullying starting with early childhood education. Clearly, bullying behavior starts as early as preschool and must be addressed as soon as it is identified. Many factors influencing bullying among school-age children play into early childhood bullying as well.

EARLY CHILDHOOD BULLYING

We are defining early childhood as birth through five years of age, the most impressionable years. "The formative early years are critical years, when traits of character are influenced and when young children gather and develop a strong sense of themselves and others," states Carol B. Hillman, author of *Before the School Bell Rings* (1995). She continues to write about the special qualities of this age—curiosity, exploration, and many lessons learned from play. "Play is the way that children learn to be in charge, to be responsible. Through play, young children gain a sense of power."

Educators in childcare programs and preschools report that they have some students who are aggressive and domineering at this early stage and ask how to distinguish a bossy child from a bullier. Bossiness crosses the line when it is affecting other children. It is also an excellent opportunity to teach young children how to stand up for themselves in an assertive way.

Another approach might be to assign a bossy child to be in charge of a project such as picking up all of the toys. The child is told to give directions to each of the other children. When the project is completed, give praise for a leadership job well done. At the same time, praise all of the children who were good followers and speak about how important it is to be both a good leader and a good follower. The bossy child should continually be given the opportunity to demonstrate that he or she is learning to be a good leader as well as a good follower.

The bottom line is that the bossy child, if his or her behavior is not nipped in the bud, may quickly become a bullier. Such children must be taught that calling classmates names, taking toys, making threats, and being too bossy are all aspects of bullying.

Young children who become bulliers often come from homes where they observe abuse, are victims of abuse, have little parental supervision, lack social skills, and experience harsh physical punishment. They often manifest antisocial behavior, signs of childhood depression, or may be very angry.

A teacher related a story that happened in her preschool. A petite bullier named Maxine had already learned how to terrorize her peers. One morning, Maxine planted herself in front of Robbie, put her hands on her hips, and emphatically told him that his mother was never going to come back for him. No words could cause more panic for a three-year-old. Robbie burst into tears. As the teacher ran over to console him, Juliet, a fellow three-year-old playmate, patted Robbie on his arm and assured him that his mommy would come and get him, just like she did every day. Robbie's tears and his bullier disappeared. At a very young age, Juliet had already become a responsible witness.

Now the teacher focused on Maxine. She was given a strong empathy lesson and experienced an appropriate consequence. Bullying has a profound effect at all stages in life, but particularly in the early years. Prevention and early intervention cannot be stressed enough.

BULLY-FREE CLASSROOMS

Early childhood educators who have very little bullying in their classrooms attribute it to the fact that they teach social skills, they teach and model kindness, and they create an environment in which the young children feel safe. It is a generally accepted fact that preschool children enter school with few, if any, social skills. They have to be taught the most basic social behavior of simply saying "please" and "thank you" at the appropriate time.

These educators meet their students at the classroom door and greet them by saying, "Good morning, Melinda" and wait for the young child to respond with "Good morning, Ms. Sunshine." The early childhood educator should encourage this very basic verbal social exchange with every student-to-student interaction and with every student-to-teacher interaction. Snack time and recess are also opportunities for teaching and practicing social skills that were taken for granted years ago. Snack time—"Please pass the cookies" and recess—"You can't say that she can't play" can teach these skills until they become second nature for young students. When students learn to respect themselves and one another at a very early age, there is no need to be a bullier.

Social skills are also learned through well-supervised "playdates." In addition, playdates help preschool children develop friendships, which in turn help build confidence.

Good social skills, friends, and confidence are all factors that deter bulliers.

POSITIVE SCHOOL ENVIRONMENT

Preschool and childcare buildings should be light, bright, and have a happy feel throughout. Children's artwork should be on the walls of the hallways as well as in the classrooms. The halls and classrooms could display posters, proverbs, and pictures of heroes. One poster we suggest would say: "Sticks and Stones Can Break Your Bones but Words Can Break Your Heart." Story time, arts and crafts, and games can be coordinated with the visuals.

Montessori educators worldwide find the peace table a very effective tool to prevent and combat bullying. On the website of The Montessori School of Tokyo (2009) we read, "Children normally find it difficult to tell us and each other how they feel. The peace table plays an important part in our classroom; two children having a disagreement will normally decide to retreat to the peace table to discuss and solve their problem. Teaching peace involves finding a way to appreciate our differences and work together more effectively than ever."

Children do well in a structured environment, one in which they know what to expect and what is expected of them. Visitors are often surprised to see the ease with which these youngsters move from one activity to the next. Some children find these transitions more difficult than others, but that is part of the teaching/learning process of early childhood education.

Parents and educators must be mindful of the fact that young children can vary as much as two years in reaching milestones. Some acquire verbal skills earlier and lag behind in motor skills and vice versa. It is important to work through their strengths to help them acquire the skills that are more challenging for them. The more confident they feel about their abilities, the less likely they will be bullied. Early intervention is crucial for their mental health and for the safety of their classmates.

MIDDLE CHILDHOOD

The developmental stages of bullying behavior progress on a continuum. Many of the behaviors exhibited by preschool children continue into kindergarten and the early elementary grades. Middle childhood is the period between the ages of six and twelve. In their book *Development Contexts in Middle Childhood* (2006), editors Aletha Huston and Marika Ripke conclude that

> although lasting individual differences are evident by the end of the preschool years, a child's developmental path in middle childhood contributes significantly to the adolescent and adult that he or she becomes. Families, peers, and the broader social and economic environment all make a difference for young people's future education, work and relationships with others.
>
> Kids in middle childhood think more abstractly, understand, for example that a person can be both nice and not nice . . . there is a kind of cognitive blooming . . . This is the time you develop industry, a sense of being able to do things, and explore things, or you develop the downside and the downside is inferiority. If you don't begin to expand your horizons and learn a lot of things, and learn the basics that school has to teach you, then you are vulnerable to long term inferiority, because you are going to feel that you can't do things.

Huston continues by pointing out "that it's not simply book learning. Its mastering the stuff we take for granted, like riding a bike, learning to swim and making friends. In fact, making friends may be one of the most important jobs of middle childhood. This is a time children really build a foundation of being able to relate to peers. Making friends, getting along with people your own age, that's critically important to your life."

Professor Huston is considered one of the leaders in the field of middle childhood. Much of her research is built on the landmark Columbia County Longitudinal Study by Leonard Eron, discussed in chapter 2.

The Eron study has been significant for many years because of its important findings as well as for the amount of subsequent research that has been conducted in the area of middle childhood. In addition to Professor Huston's findings we have the work of Dr. Eric F. Dubow, professor of psychology at Bowling Green State University and an adjunct researcher at the University of Michigan. Professor Dubow and a team of researchers at the University of Michigan conducted an extensive analysis of the Eron study (2009). In an interview with the *Toledo Blade* about the Columbia Company Longitudinal Study, professor Dubow was quoted: "It's obviously not true for every child, but a child's behavior at age 8 is relatively predictive of behavior in adolescence, and that in turn predicts educational status . . . It is the impact of aggressive behavior on educational status that appears to lead to low occupational success." Thus, the continuum from early childhood to middle childhood continues into adolescence and adulthood.

"This study and others like it come out of a growing awareness among psychologists, educators and policy makers that this period known as middle childhood between the ages of 6 and 12, has a far greater impact on making us who we are than earlier theorists acknowledged," wrote Jenni Laidman, Blade Science Writer in her November 2006 article "Is Age 8 Too Late? Kids Who Don't Play Well with Others May Not Be Successful Adults."

The results of this ongoing research affirm the importance of understanding and developing effective techniques for prevention and early intervention. There is increasing information that both bulliers and popular students can become targets.

Megan, who is now in her fifties, recalled very clearly for us the influence of going from being popular to being bullied had on her life. She was very popular in eighth grade, and then in ninth grade she became the target of a bullier "who was much bigger than I was and who fought me to the ground. To this day I have no idea of why she chose me to be her victim." Megan went on to graduate from a prestigious university, pursued a number of careers, and had several meaningful relationships but never married. Her adult life included numerous periods of severe depression, which she connected to her change in status, confusion, and fear in the ninth grade.

INTERNET BULLYING STARTS EARLY

A new phrase has entered our vocabulary—Barbie Brats. "The name applies to an overlooked group of kids—young children, only 6 or 8 or 10 years old, who bully other kids in real life or on the Internet," reports Louise Mysilk, LCSW (2008). She also indicates that bullying among younger elementary-school-age children is on the rise. Studies show that three-quarters of children aged eight to eleven say they have been bullied on the Internet.

The fact that Internet bullying starts at such a young age must be a real wake-up call for parents, educators, school administrators, and mental health professionals. Middle childhood classrooms should have class rules agreed upon by the students at the beginning of the school year. A teacher-led discussion gives the students an opportunity to contribute to the rules and consequences and take ownership of them. Three to five rules seem to work best and should include the concepts of respect and responsibility. This process and enforcement are very effective for the creation of bully-free elementary-school classrooms.

Montessori schools find the peace table very effective for middle child-hood students as well as for the preschool students. The students report that just the opportunity "to talk things through" is very helpful.

MIDDLE-SCHOOL BULLYING

Bullying peaks at middle school, when students are eleven to fourteen. Some middle schools begin with the sixth grade, some with seventh. Regardless, it can be a treacherous time of life. As one student said: "Middle school is senselessly evil."

The physical, emotional, and sexual development of students varies greatly. One student can be four feet and another two feet taller. With their hormones leaping all over the place, middle-school students are on an emotional roller coaster. They are moving toward independence but are still in limbo.

The American Academy of Child and Adolescent Psychiatry says that this stage is a time of experimentation, testing limits, and a struggle for a sense of identity. These students' intellectual interests expand but at this age have limited thoughts of the future. They are awkward about their changing bodies and have an increased interest in sex.

All of this angst leads to thrashing around and lashing out at their peers. The taunting can be outrageous and relentless. Sexual bullying, especially around sexual language, is rampant and causes enormous pain.

The adults in authority at middle school must keep a vigilant eye on the way students tyrannize each other. There is nothing more devastating for an adolescent male than to have his masculinity publicly challenged.

At the beginning of the school year, we advise that bullying in all of its forms be addressed, especially cyberbullying, and it must be made clear that it will not be tolerated. Spell out the consequences and how they will be enforced. Don't forget this is a time for testing limits—the sooner you make a rule, the sooner it will be challenged. Every adult must intervene at the first infraction and maintain authority throughout the year.

At the same time, keep in mind these young people are searching for adults in whom they can confide. They have just left being in the embrace of one teacher a year for six years and now they are simply one part of a mass. In conversations with teachers at this level, we learn that they work very hard to find a balance between being a sounding board and being firmly in control of the classroom. One teacher advises: "Don't show it when you're shocked and don't get into a power struggle. Don't ever call them "children"—that word grates. They love humor and appreciate honesty."

Above all, keep them safe. Middle school can be a very dangerous place and they desperately need your protection.

HIGH-SCHOOL BULLYING

"According to recent studies, between 20–40 percent of U.S. teen-agers report being bullied three or more times during the last year. Between 7–15 percent report bullying others three or more times during the past year," writes Debbie Wilborn (2008).

She indicates that compared to nonbullying teens, bulliers tend to:

* Have difficulty accepting criticism
* Have the need to be the center of attention
* Be more likely to drink alcohol and use drugs excessively
* Be at greater risk of being victimized themselves (about 50 percent of bulliers are also victims at some point)
* Be at higher risk for mental health problems such as conduct disorder and attention deficit hyperactivity disorder
* Be more likely to be antisocial in adulthood
* Be more likely to use violence in relationships
* Be more likely to get into trouble with the law.

Wilborn continues, reporting that compared to nonbullied teens, targets tend to:

* Be at higher risk for mental and physical health problems such as depression, stomachaches, and headaches
* Be absent from school more frequently because of bullying
* Continue to experience higher levels of anxiety through adulthood
* Have low self-worth
* Feel that control of their lives rests with someone else.

Research indicates that a majority of adolescents do not feel safe in school. These students maintain that teachers and other school personnel have "no clue" as to how much bullying behavior goes on every day in the hallways and other nonacademic venues such as locker rooms, school grounds, and buses.

Although bullying may decrease during the senior-high-school years, it is certainly more violent. Most shootings occur at high schools. With the statistics related above it is no wonder that students don't feel safe in school.

Warning Signs for the Adolescent

* Shows a significant personality change and/or change in behavior
* Has a significant change in sleeping and/or eating habits
* Expresses fear about going to school
* Refuses to go to school

* Talks about suicide
* Attempts suicide or other forms of physical harm to self

ADOLESCENT DATING ABUSE

Adolescent dating abuse is certainly a serious manifestation of teen peer abuse. It has become a matter of such serious concern that loveisrespect.org (the National Teen Dating Abuse Helpline) reports the following "dating abuse fast facts" based on findings of a March 2006 study commissioned by Liz Claiborne, Inc.:

* One in five teens who have been in a serious relationship report being hit, slapped, or pushed by a partner.
* One in three girls who have been in a serious relationship say they've been concerned about being physically hurt by their partner.
* One in four teens who have been in a serious relationship say their boyfriend or girlfriend has tried to prevent them from spending time with friends or family; the same number have been pressured to only spend time with their partner.
* One in three girls between the ages of sixteen and eighteen say sex is expected for people of their age if they're in a relationship; half of the teen girls who have experienced sexual pressure report they are afraid the relationship would break up if they did not give in.
* Nearly one in four girls in a relationship (23 percent) reported going further sexually than they wanted as a result of pressure.

These facts demand our immediate attention. Parents, teachers, and health professionals are urged to heed the following warning signs:

* Changes in teen's mood and/or personality
* Mental health issues such as depression and/or anxiety
* Withdrawal from family and friends in response to boyfriend's/girlfriend's demand to control their time
* No longer interested in hobbies or other activities that were previously of great interest
* Expressions of jealousy
* Strong students whose grades are obviously falling
* Unexplained injuries should never be ignored
* Name-calling and put-downs in public and private
* Display of anger and violent behavior such as punching, grabbing, pushing, slapping, hitting, shoving
* Same type of name calling we see in all types of peer abuse: put-downs, making the partner feel bad about herself/himself, telling their partner

that no one else would date her/him or that they are ugly or fat or stupid . . . and on and on.

Parents or a significant adult in the adolescent's life must teach the teen to ask herself/himself the following questions:

Do you strike out at your girlfriend/boyfriend?
Does s/he make you feel uncomfortable in any way?
Does s/he demand that you change your behavior to keep her/him happy?
Do you have a problem controlling your anger?
Have you hit or hurt someone you care about?

It is imperative that adolescents in abusive relationships get protection and help immediately. It is also imperative to engage students to take action in their own behalf.

An amazing conference about bullying, "When Push Comes to Shove—Finding Solutions to Bullying Behavior," took place in Topeka, Kansas, in early 2009 and Fried was a keynote speaker. The goal was to empower high-school students to become advocates for change in their own schools. January Scott, Conference Coordinator, recruited students from all over the community to attend and thirty student leaders from three high schools and one middle school were trained prior to the conference to be small-group facilitators.

One hundred and twenty adults, including principals, counselors, teachers, and parents, and 118 students came together to integrate information they had learned from keynote speakers and make commitments to make a difference upon their return to their schools. The evaluations indicated that the students left the conference with changed perspectives about the seriousness of bullying. They felt a greater compassion for students who were bullied, a deeper commitment to intervene when their friends were bullying, and they were highly motivated to become more involved in bullying prevention.

When students take ownership of peer abuse, the pain can stop.

OFFENSE	SY0405	SY0506	SY0607
BAT	50	46	16
DIS	503	2982	666
DRS	381	192	117
FIT	58	141	62
GRA	0	9	5
HRS	82	243	110
INS	141	689	180
PRC	90	209	100
PRO	57	274	111
SXH	10	5	2
TRE	33	43	12
WPO	2	19	5
Total Incidents	1407	4852	1386
Total Student Pop	782	1292	977
BAT	Battery		
DIS	Disruption		
DRS	Disrespect		
FIT	Fighting		
GRA	Gang Related Act		
HRS	Horseplay		
INS	Insubordination		
PRC	Peer Conflict		
PRO	Profanity		
SXH	Sexual Harassment		
TRE	Threat/Intimidation		
WPO	Weapons Poss		

8

Helping Students with Special Needs Achieve Success

"Every day is a battle for me. I wish I didn't have all these problems. Why can't they just leave me alone?"

—Stewart, a special needs student

Given all that special needs students have to deal with they certainly don't need to be forced to deal with bullies as well. Yet people who are different often become the targets of bullies and special needs students are frequently perceived as different.

They might be gifted and talented, learning disabled, twice exceptional, autistic, ADD, ADHD, visually or hearing impaired. In many classrooms there are students who are very protective of their special needs classmates but in some classrooms bullies try to take over.

Early diagnosis and intervention for a disease like cancer can result in a cure or long-term remission. Early diagnosis and intervention cannot cure learning disabilities. There is no known cure for learning disabilities. However, the route to productivity for students with learning disabilities depends on early detection and appropriate intervention.

Just a few examples of famous people who were able to compensate for their disabilities: Dyslexia – Presidents George Washington and Woodrow Wilson, Tom Cruise, Patricia Palacco, and Vice-President Nelson Rockefeller who is said to have memorized every speech because of his concern about his inability to read the words. Learning Disability – Winston Churchill, Walt Disney, Alexander Graham Bell, and Thomas Edison, who didn't learn to read until he was 12 years old. Downs syndrome – Chris Burke; Hearing Impaired – Marlee Matlin; Manic-depressive – Patty Duke.

A graphic example of an individual who was able to compensate for his disability is Jim Abbott who was born without one hand and yet was able to win Olympic gold in 1988 and became an outstanding major league pitcher. We could share literally hundreds of stories about famous people who learned to compensate for their disabilities and made outstanding contributions to humanity. We encourage you to go onto the Internet and input "famous people with disabilities" to read some of the fascinating stories about these famous individuals, and in some cases how they suffered at the hands of bullies.

Bullies don't usually target confident classmates. Helping special needs students succeed and eliminating their "differentness" is vital to reducing the target population of bullies. That is why early diagnosis and intervention is so important to teach these students how to compensate for their disabilities.

As mentioned earlier we must acknowledge that there are children who are more likely to become bullies because of inborn traits, such as those who were crack babies, who suffered from fetal alcohol syndrome, and some children with attention deficit disorder (ADD) or attention deficit hyperactivity disorder (ADHD) whose disruptive behavior patterns may have a biological basis. They often become targets as well.

Provocative targets create tension by irritating and annoying others and are more likely to fight back when attacked. Provocative targets may have ADHD, Asperger's syndrome, or learning disabilities that prevent them from picking up on social cues other children intuitively understand. These children can irritate others without even realizing it. Many parents have moved their children with special needs from one school to another, year after year, because of their ongoing pain. These children are extraordinarily bright and talented in many ways but suffer from inborn traits that they have not been able to control.

THE MEDICATION DEBATE

Ritalin makes it possible for some of these children to accommodate to the classroom environment, control their actions and interactions, and contain bullying behavior. Two widely used drugs, Concerta and Adderall XR, last twelve to fourteen hours and spare children the embarrassment of leaving the classroom to receive a dose of Ritalin, which lasts only four or five hours.

While the majority of families with children who are diagnosed with ADD or ADHD are grateful for the benefits of these drugs, it is important to recognize that there has been much concern expressed about medicating some children unnecessarily. Numerous articles have illustrated cases where parents preferred to "drugulate" their children's behavior rather than deal with the causes. We have interviewed several pediatricians who report seeing "miracles occur" with patients who are correctly diagnosed and appropriate medication prescribed.

Some parents of children with ADD or ADHD are finding a therapeutic element in karate and other forms of martial arts. Many doctors support this idea, as do several national nonprofit resource groups for people with the disorder, including the National Attention Deficit Disorder Association and Children and Adults with Attention-Deficit/Hyperactivity Disorder. They say that such courses help ease the symptoms of the disorder: impulsiveness, inability to concentrate, and, in some cases, hyperactivity. Other experts who say that it is nothing more than wishful thinking, however, dismiss this theory. They point to a lack of medical evidence to back up the theory.

MAJOR CONCERN ABOUT BULLYING OF SPECIAL NEEDS STUDENTS

The depth of concern about the abuse of special needs students is underscored by the wide range of participants in sessions on bullying which Sosland conducts at the annual state conference of the Missouri Learning Disabilities Association. Parents and educators from the field of early childhood education through high school come to these sessions eager for information to help their special needs students. Parents come expressing frustration with teachers and administrators who ignore their plea for help. Others share triumphs. Educators include classroom teachers, administrators, resource teachers, and mental health professionals who express growing concern about the marked increase in bullying they observe, particularly cyber-bullying. They are also looking for guidance on how to deal with parents of bullies. Strategies for children who have special needs to deal with bullies are listed in Chapter 8, "Change Agents," under the heading "Special Education Teachers."

CORRECT DIAGNOSIS

In many cases special needs students' needs are not identified and diagnosed. This often leads to unnecessary frustration and failure in the classroom. Unknowing parents will often say to them, "I know you can do it, if you would just try harder" but this just makes matters worse because it continues to make the students feel like failures. In the meantime, it makes them more apt to be targets of bullies.

The way to break this cycle is to prove to these students that they can be successful. We learned this important lesson from an eighth grade student, Candy, who was reading at the third grade level when we first met her in a middle school that was formerly a feeder school to a distinguished college-prep public high school. As the neighborhood changed students entered the middle school from low income, non-college educated households.

The faculty refused to change the curriculum to meet the needs of the student body. As one teacher put it, "I have always taught *Animal Farm* in eighth grade and I will continue to do so," even though some of her students were reading at the third grade level. She was teaching but her students were not learning and they were cutting class.

The school was located in a commercial area and some of the students were actually shoplifting. The shop owners got together, pooled some money and came to the University Reading Education Department to ask for help. As a result, we developed a sixteen-week program where we met with small groups of students for one hour twice a week, teaching them the basic reading skills that they had missed.

Three-Step Process

In conjunction with this project, we designed a three-step process – observation, evaluation and intervention. The first step was teacher observation. Teachers were asked to observe the students and refer those students who might best benefit from our program. Next we evaluated each student and established his or her respective instructional levels and then we began our intervention.

The students gained an average of two years in their reading levels during the sixteen-week program, which is true of similar programs as well. We asked the student who started at the third grade level and scored at the eighth grade level by the end of the program how she managed such an increase. Her response was "You showed me that I could learn to read. I had given up on ever improving my reading skills but each week I got better in the work I did with you. I realized I could learn, and I did". We were so impressed with her achievement we followed up with her in high school and found that she was continuing to experience success at grade level.

Annie's Story

We received a call at the University from a fourth grade teacher inquiring whether we had an education major who might tutor one of her students who wasn't learning to read even though she was being taught at a second reading level. The teacher told us that she had requested a battery of tests for Annie because she was puzzled by her lack of progress learning to read. She questioned the results, which pegged Annie's IQ score as a slow learner, which is why she called us.

We checked Annie's record and found that she had had a battery of tests in first grade and at that time her IQ was average and she had been diagnosed with a learning disability. For some reason, Annie's learning disability had not been addressed, and academically, she fell further and further behind each year.

We asked Annie's teacher how she knew that Annie was not a slow learner and she replied, " I have been teaching for fifteen years and I could tell by looking into her eyes. I have had enough students who are slow learners and they have a dull look which was not true of Annie." This is a graphic example of the efficacy of teacher observation." One of our students accepted the assignment to tutor Annie but before she began, she gave Annie a reading evaluation, Step Two of our process. The evaluation indicated that Annie was reading at the pre-primer level and not at the second grade level.

Step Three, the intervention process, began when our student started to re-teach Annie at the appropriate pre-primer level. Annie quickly advanced with each tutoring session. Our student's evaluation of Annie allowed her to address Annie's learning disability at the appropriate instructional level, an important key to success.

Tools for Evaluation—The Informal Reading Inventory

One of the best tools for evaluating reading levels is the Informal Reading Inventory, which can be administered within 12-15 minutes and allows the teacher, clinician or parent who does the administration to observe the student in the process of reading. The Inventory establishes the student's Independent Reading Level, that level at which the student can read without assistance, the Instructional Level, that level at which the student should be taught, and the Frustration level, that level at which the student should NEVER be taught. The Listening Capacity is the final level, which measures the student's achievement potential, once the reading disability is addressed.

Reading is a skill that must be practiced just like any other skill, tennis, basketball, or piano. The Independent Reading Level is that level at which a student should practice reading, and read for pleasure. The Instructional Level is the appropriate level to teach reading skills commensurate with the student's intellectual capacity. Annie, unfortunately, was being taught at her Frustration Level, which is why she was not able to learn. Finally, Annie's Listening Capacity was at the fifth grade reading level even though she was in the fourth grade. Looking back at her history we found that she had been retained one year and really should have been in the fifth grade. It is obvious that she had the capacity to do grade level work with the proper intervention. Annie almost fell through the cracks but a talented teacher rescued her. We urge parents to be strong advocates for their children if they feel that they might be falling through the cracks.

An Assessment of Letter Name Knowledge

Another very simple instrument for evaluation of students with learning disabilities is a test of letter names, upper case and lower case. The student is asked to read the letters that are not in alphabetical order. Directions for the administration are found in Appendix D. In a special project at the Juvenile Justice Center, Sosland gave a battery of reading instruments to 20 seventh grade boys. Five of the 20 could not read all the letters on the test of alphabet knowledge and of course their reading levels on the Informal Reading Inventory were very low. Sosland often described these results in her classes and one student who had a son in a suburban high school who continued to experience difficulty reading, administered this test to her son only to discover that he, indeed, could not read all the letters.

During the time that we were writing this book Sosland had a referral by a parent of a first grader who was experiencing difficulty learning to read. A test of letter names indicated that he had not mastered the letters of the alphabet, ending the alphabet song with the letter order "wyvxuz." He also confused b/d and p/q, common errors but which need to be corrected before a student can learn to read competently. Parents and teachers should not assume that a first grader has mastered the alphabet and are urged to use the simple test of letter names to assess mastery of the alphabet.

Tom, Sosland's first student at the University Reading Clinic was a seventh grader reading at the fourth grade level. He was one of seven children, all high academic achievers so his reading problems created emotional problems as well. In addition, his older brother, a source of pain, which he discussed in each tutoring session, taunted him mercilessly. Sosland discovered very quickly that he confused the letters g and j. Once she re-taught these two letters, she was able to re-teach other reading skills and the student began to enjoy reading. By practicing at his Independent Reading Level, he was able to read at grade level within a year. Tom progressed from the fourth grade level to the eighth grade level by the time he entered eighth grade. When this occurred, the sibling stopped the taunting.

Wepman Test of Auditory Discrimination

Another key component to assure reading competence, that is the foundation on which academic success is built, is auditory discrimination. The Wepman Test of Auditory Discrimination is very easy to administer and students really enjoy doing this exercise.

Finally, we would recommend a Multiple Intelligences Inventory. Students enjoy taking this Inventory and it allows intervention to take place working through the student's strengths. There are more that 700 Multiple Intelligences Inventories available on the Internet. Readers are encouraged to select one that is appropriate for their student or child.

This battery of instruments can be administered in the classroom and provides a wealth of information for students, parents and teachers. The information will enable a program of intervention to be available for the special needs student even if they don't qualify for special services.

Individualized Attention

Students like Candy, Annie and the boys at the Juvenile Justice Center who have fallen so far behind must have individualized instruction, be taught at their appropriate Instructional Level and develop their academic skills through Independent practice.

Individualized instruction can take place with one-on-one tutoring. Student tutors from nearby colleges and universities, peer tutors and adult volunteers are all valuable personal resources that have proven to be very successful. The tutoring sessions are very important but equally important is the Independent practice that will only happen when students are motivated to succeed. We have come full circle to Candy's lesson about showing - not telling -students who are failing, that they can learn.

Dr. Sidney Pakula, a revered pediatrician in Kansas City for many decades, told Sosland that he saw a thousand cases of reading problems in his practice each year. After he and a number of colleagues referred these patients for educational evaluation for many years, they decided to develop a screening instrument for pediatricians to administer in their own offices. This was during the period of "the great debate over phonics versus whole word instruction."

"Dr. Pakula and his colleagues discovered that most of the students who were experiencing difficulty learning to read, were in classrooms where instruction did not match their learning mode. Some students were being taught to read in a phonics program who would have done better with a whole word approach and some students who were in classes using the whole word approach, were much more successful when taught using a phonics approach. Today, we recommend using an eclectic approach that combines phonics and the whole word approach to reading instruction.

There is much to be learned from countries abroad. Linda Darling-Hammond, a professor Education at Stanford University, has collected valuable research about the extent of resources that are being poured into teacher training and support in Asia, Australia, New Zealand, Canada, Finland, Sweden, Norway, and the Netherlands.

They are prepared more extensively and are well-paid in relation to competing occupations. All teacher candidates in Finland, Sweden, Norway and the Netherlands receive two to three years of graduate level preparation for teaching, at government expense, plus a living stipend.

Finland has been a poster child for school improvement. Teachers learn how to create programs that engage students in research and inquiry on a regular basis. There, training focuses on how to teach students who learn in different ways – including those with special needs.

Parent Advocacy

Parents need to be aware of the type of instruction their children are receiving. In some cases the nature of the delivery of instruction does not match the child's learning style that causes an academic problem, which then creates a child with special needs, and can snowball into a bullying situation.

Over the years Sosland has had a number of referrals for educational evaluation by parents of kindergartners who reported that their young children who had been toilet trained for two to three years were suddenly bedwetting. In one case the parents realized that the bedwetting stopped when they were out of town for spring break and away from school. These were all very bright children who found themselves in kindergarten situations that were highly stressful, including bullying.

All the bullying literature, at all levels, stresses the importance of communication with your children. This is easier during the early years as opposed to adolescence, but if it can be maintained throughout the child rearing years, parents will be able to intervene on their children's behalf when necessary. Red flags, such as a return of bedwetting, loss of appetite, or stomach aches when it is time to leave for school should be heeded immediately.

Twice-exceptional Students

Although the term "at-risk students" has been used to describe a variety of the school population, it is most commonly used to identify low achievers who are "at-risk" of becoming dropouts, who may become adolescent suicides, participate in substance abuse and become teen-age parents. Then there are students who are "at-risk" precisely because they are overlooked as being "at-risk." These students are both learning disabled and gifted/academically talented. They are twice-exceptional.

The learning disability may mask the academic talent and the academic talent may mask the learning disability. These students often appear to be average or labeled as underachievers. There is no fault with being average but when a student who is twice-exceptional is mislabeled as average, neither the special needs of the learning disability nor of the giftedness is met.

One of the most common deficits that may "mask" the ability of a bright student is that of fine motor control, which interferes with the ability to get ideas from the head to the paper. Some students have difficulty remembering how to form the letters while others have difficulty using the muscles necessary for handwriting. In any case, the word processor has been a helpful tool for some of these students; others have used the tape recorder to help them compensate for their disabilities.

These students often become behavior problems in the classroom. For example, Jon, a second grader in a private school was acting out and very disruptive in class. Teachers and administrators attributed his behavior to "being the youngest very spoiled child" in an upper income family. However his parents insisted that Jon have an educational evaluation and these test results indicated that Jon was reading at the eighth grade level but was being taught from a second grade basal reading program. He also had a subtle fine motor problem that kept him from completing writing assignments to his teacher's satisfaction.

Giving Jon eighth level reading material and adjusting for his fine motor skills deficit eliminated his negative behavior within a week. How long could any student, or adult for that matter, endure reading six levels below what he was capable of reading in class day after day without acting out in frustration? Clearly, the behavior was a cry for help, which Jon, fortunately, received. Acting-out behavior in class and/or at home often is another red flag that should alert adults to a student's special needs problem. It is imperative to respond to the symptom by looking for the cause of the behavior.

Fine motor deficits caused academic problems for Edward, a bright highschool student. He was being tutored in math because he continued to fail the math quizzes. Edward insisted that he understood the math concepts, though he was unable to pass the tests. When Edward's mother checked with the math teacher, the instructor confirmed her son's mastery of the math concepts in spite of his test scores.

The mother tried, to no avail, to persuade the teacher to take the student's fine motor issues into consideration. The teacher refused, on the grounds that "it wouldn't be fair to the other students." The mother countered "But the other students don't have a learning disability!" Over the years as we have advocated for individual special needs students from preschool through graduate school we have been told, "But it wouldn't be fair to the other students." In each case we have repeated, "But the other students don't have a learning disability" and tried to explain the need to help the students to compensate for that disability. Any educator from early childhood through graduate school who doesn't know or understand the difference between special needs students and regular students should not be in any classroom. This lack of professionalism underscores the importance of placing well prepared educators in our schools advocated by those who are calling for school reform. We owe this to our students and to ensure a welleducated population for the future of our country.

Edward's experience raised the important question of whether we are test-ing for understanding and knowledge or for the ability to write a quiz. If teachers understand the fact that among students there is a certain popula-tion who have deficits for which they must compensate we can avoid many problems for these students.

Some twice-exceptional students may be ADHD, discussed earlier in this chapter. Others may have language disorders, which interfere with their ability to follow oral instructions, auditory lessons presented orally or expressing themselves orally. There are students who manifest just the opposite problem, that of spatial orientation who have difficulty process-ing information visually. These are often the students who make brilliant contributions to classroom discussions but experience reading difficulties. Some students may have difficulty retrieving information from memory.

Sequencing problems often lead bright students to experience difficulty, as does a lack of organizational skills. These same students have intellectual capacities that place them in the gifted and talented range. They often have very large vocabularies, may have been early readers, and have unusual language skills. Some of these students have long attention spans, unusual persistence and concentration. They learn quickly and retain vast amounts of information. These students require far less practice to master learning. They think deeply, are creative, have a broad range of varied interests, are curious, and willing to take risks and experiment.

This is just a very brief overview of the types of deficits bright students may experience that then makes them twice-exceptional. How do we meet the special learning needs of these unique students?

A Special Teacher Meets Special Needs

Pat Antonopoulos, a kindergarten teacher in a suburban school district did an Independent Research project with Sosland to try to answer this ques-tion. She developed what she called "The Center Approach" to meet the diverse needs of 46 children ranging in chronological age from 5.1 years to 6.2 years and an I.Q. range of 82 to 164. The morning session of the kin-dergarten had 24 students and the afternoon session had 22 students. Each center had activities that encouraged creativity for all developmental levels. The activities also encouraged logical thinking, information processing and detail recall. Many of the activities are verbal, easily accomplished with few materials and exciting for the children.

Centers, also known as Learning Centers, give teachers the opportunity to teach to their students' strengths and give students the opportunity to make choices. Centers can be designed for individual work or group activities.

For the early childhood classroom we recommend a Literacy Center where children can curl up with a book or practice writing their letters, an

Art Center, a Drama Center with dress up clothes, a Science Center, sand and water table, and many preschools now have a computer in each classroom. Some children tend to favor one center. If that is the case, teacher guidance usually encourages the student to try other centers as well.

Similar centers are created by teachers in middle childhood classes on a more advanced level. Incorporation of Learning Centers varies from classroom to classroom depending on the teacher's approach to teaching.

These centers allow each student to function at his/her ability level. At the end of the school year each child thought that he/she was Mrs. Antonopoulos' favorite student and each child felt successful. This kindergarten teacher said she would never go back to her former way of teaching. Her work was cutting edge some twenty years ago but has proven to help all students, at all grade levels, including special needs students achieve success over these many years.

Gifted and Talented Students

Unusually gifted and talented students also have special needs. We tend to equate special needs only with children who are physically, academically, or neurologically challenged, but gifted and talented children deserve extra attention, especially when it comes to bullying. More than two-thirds of academically talented eighth graders say they have been bullied at school and nearly one-third harbored violent thoughts as a result, according to a study believed to be the first to examine the prevalence and impact of bullying in a group some experts regard as particularly vulnerable.

The study, published in the *Gifted Child Quarterly* (2006), involved 432 students in eleven states who had been identified by their school systems as gifted. Jean Sunde Peterson, an associate professor at Purdue University, sought to explore whether harassing behavior affected gifted children differently:

> All children are affected adversely by bullying, but gifted children differ from other children in significant ways. Many are intense, sensitive and stressed by their own and others' high expectations and their ability, interests and behavior may make them more vulnerable. Additionally, social justice issues are very important them and they struggle to make sense of cruelty and aggression.

One of the most alarming findings of the research involved the frequency of violent thoughts. By eighth grade, approximately 37 percent of boys and 23 percent of girls in the study reported having unspecified violent thoughts in response to being bullied; 11 percent admitted that they resorted to violence.

Gifted students are frequently the object of derision and isolation by their peers for many reasons, such as jealousy and perceived differences. Reinforcing our concern about children who turn their pain inward is the example of J. Daniel Scruggs, a slightly built Connecticut middle-schooler with an IQ of 139. When he could no longer cope with the relentless abuse he received from his classmates, including making him eat his lunch off of the cafeteria floor, he chose to commit suicide.

Gifted students tend to bully themselves. They put enormous pressure on themselves to maintain their exceedingly high standards. This causes high levels of stress and anxiety, even physical extremes such as heart palpitations and fainting. These students require special support to conquer the issues they experience.

Allise was fortunate to have a school counselor, Mrs. Nikki Currie, who created "Tool Boxes" for a number of high-achieving students. Each student had their own Tool Box that included unique contents to help them calm down. Allise was given breathing exercises that she could focus on when she began to feel nervous. Mrs. Currie told her to count her breaths and use accompanying hand signs that wouldn't be obvious to others. If that didn't work, she suggested that Allise scratch her ankles, because it's harder to faint when your head is below your heart. Additionally, Mrs. Currie signed a permanent pass for Allise that she could use to leave her classroom, when necessary, knowing that Allise would never abuse the privilege.

More than the amazing solutions that continued to surface for each new challenge was the constancy that the counselor represented. She never doubted that there wasn't a way to handle each predicament and her students knew that she would find it, somehow. The spirit of confidence she radiated to them was indispensable.

We hope this information will inspire parents, teachers, and university students to become strong advocates for these special students who often become targets of bulliers. Working in synchrony, we can break the cycle of pain, rage, and revenge.

9

The Challenge of Changing the Culture

"I think if everyone stopped bullying it would be a lot funner place to be."

—Jimmy, a student

CHANGING THE CULTURE: THREE LITTLE WORDS, ONE ENORMOUS CHALLENGE.

Many years ago, a workshop leader at a public-health conference described a public-health approach to addressing community problems. The workshop presenter related the story of a village where many of the people had dysentery. Two approaches were being considered. The individual approach was to treat every person who had an intestinal disorder, the second was a community approach—to invest in a sewer system.

The bullying disorder that ravages many of our schools requires both approaches. We must find a way to identify and treat the infected children, both the targets and the bulliers who are in pain. At the same time, we must create the equivalent of a sewer system to address the *source* of the problem, which is to change the culture of the school community. This chapter focuses on the latter approach.

There is much that we can learn from Malcolm Gladwell's book *The Tipping Point* (2002). In his book, Gladwell talks about the factors involved when a particular idea or trend becomes contagious, when it bursts out of its contained state and spreads like a virus. He refers to this mysterious transformation as an epidemic. He is fascinated by the one dramatic moment in an epidemic when everything can change all at once and becomes the Tipping Point.

Consider bullying as it relates to Gladwell's observation. How does a particular school atmosphere encourage mean-spirited behavior? At what point do a few students pick up on cues that encourage them to bully freely and become a determining factor in the level of accepted cruelty? Even more importantly, how can a school where bullying has become an epidemic rally to create an atmosphere where it is "cool to be kind" rather than "cool to be cruel?"

THREE AGENTS OF CHANGE

Gladwell claims that there are three agents of change—the Law of the Few, the Stickiness Factor, and the Power of Context. The Law of the Few demonstrates the power of a few people to set an epidemic into motion—a disease epidemic or a social epidemic, a negative epidemic or a positive one. An example of a negative disease epidemic would be the flu epidemic of 1918, which was first observed in the spring of that year. Had it been contained originally, when the first cases were diagnosed, the results might have been different, but by the end of the year its effects had caused the deaths of between twenty and forty million people worldwide.

To illustrate his claim, Gladwell points to a few people who have the capacity to set a social epidemic in motion. A most celebrated example of word-of-mouth contagion is Paul Revere. Astride his horse, he traveled thirteen miles in two hours and knocked on doors in every town along the way. His famous warning: "The British are coming" was heeded by local leaders who spread the word. By the time the British arrived, they were met with fierce resistance.

A most intriguing fact is that a man named William Dawes set out with the same message in a different direction but for the most part he was ignored. Why? Dawes didn't have the social standing and credibility that Revere did. This piece of information is very relevant when we relate Gladwell's account to our concerns about bullying and the power of a few respected students to change the bullying culture.

We offer another example of a positive social epidemic. It is the cultural revolution that occurred around smoking. There was a time when smoking was considered to be kind of sexy and romantic. The health issues were not yet exposed and the tobacco industry had a grip on public consumption with its expertly crafted marketing techniques.

The amazing shift prompted by lawsuits, personal decisions, and policies banning smoking in public areas is absolutely phenomenal. Who would have imagined that smoking—an imbedded behavior pattern and even an addiction for some—could be prohibited in public spaces? The shift, championed by only a few in the beginning, brought about a dramatic change in our society.

The Stickiness Factor that Gladwell identifies looks at the elements that cause a message to stay with us rather than go in one ear and out the other.

A most interesting example was an experiment conducted by the social psychologist Howard Levanthal in the 1960s and reported by Gladwell. His goal was to persuade a group of college seniors at Yale University to get a free tetanus shot.

The students were divided into groups and given different booklets. One booklet was a "high-fear" version, indicating all the possible consequences if a tetanus shot was not received, including vivid photographs of catheters, tubes, and wounds. Another booklet, the "low-fear" version had no photographs, and the verbal imagery was toned down considerably.

When Levanthal looked at the results of how many students had actually gone to the health center to obtain shots, a mere 3 percent had taken action. Neither approach had "stuck." When they redid the experiment and included a map of the campus with the health center circled and the times that the shots were available, 28 percent of the students took advantage of the inoculation. The Stickiness Factor occurred when the information that was given was both practical and personal. According to Gladwell, for the Stickiness Factor to transfer to an epidemic, "ideas have to be memorable and move us to action." So it is with bullying. We must mobilize students with stories that touch them and solutions within their reach.

The last of Gladwell's agents of change is the Power of Context. A sterling example is the Broken Windows theory, referenced in *The Tipping Point*, which was the brainchild of criminologists James Q. Wilson and George Kelling in 1982. They maintain that when a sense of disorder in a community is prevalent—such as broken windows that aren't repaired, graffiti that isn't erased, and litter that isn't picked up, vandals will feel freer to abuse the rights of others. The residents will perceive that no one cares and no one is in charge. Perception has a strong influence on behavior.

Wilson and Kelling recommend that little problems be repaired as soon as possible. Their premise is that an epidemic can be reversed when attention is paid to the smallest details.

An amazing example is the city of New York in the early 1990s. When Rudolph Giuliani became Mayor, he appointed William Bratton as Chief of the New York City Police Department. Bratton, a believer in the Broken Windows theory, decided to crack down on fare-beating and arrest the people who were cheating the system. He went after squeegee-wielding panhandlers and took on eradicating graffiti and litter. His strategy worked. His methods were successful and New York City experienced a 50 percent reduction in crime and a notable increase in cleanliness—a legendary transformation.

This argument for taking care of problems when they first arise is especially relevant to dealing with bullying behaviors immediately. When discipline is lax, it gives the message that you can torment your classmates with impunity.

The Law of the Few

Pulling together Gladwell's three agents of change as a strategy to change the school culture begins with the Law of the Few. It makes good sense to gather a cadre of students who carry significant influence with their peers and leverage their leadership. Julie Dombo, a school counselor at Haysville Middle School in Kansas created a Natural Helpers program in 1997 that trains twenty eighth-grade students to become role models and mentors to sixth-grade students. The Natural Helpers are nominated and selected by their peers in the spring of their seventh-grade year. One of their projects was conducting a Pink Shirt campaign. The concept came from a report in Canada where a boy who wore a pink shirt to school was razzed and called sexual names. The next day a whole group of boys came to his defense by wearing pink shirts.

This program was kicked off in September by a school assembly where Fried spoke and the Natural Helpers all wore pink T-shirts. They acted out skits that demonstrated bullying situations and showed how the situations could be solved by students. Fried worked with the Natural Helpers following the assembly, and during the course of the year the Natural Helpers made themselves available to be good listeners and tutors, encouraged positive behavior, and defused conflicts between students.

Testimony to their impact came halfway through the year when a group of mean-spirited girls began bullying a girl who always wore a bow in her hair. One day the clique of hurtful girls came to school wearing bows in their hair as a form of ridicule. The Natural Helpers inspiration served as stimulus and through word of mouth, a small but highly visible number of students came to school the next day wearing bows in their hair, including countless boys! By the end of the day, as the idea caught on, more and more students found ways to participate. Even teachers, both male and female, appeared with bows. The clique of mean girls became quite contrite and their bullying stopped. Such is the Law of the Few.

The Stickiness Factor

What messages can we convey to bullies, targets, and witnesses that will have an impact? In the world of bullying, the Stickiness Factor has a strong connection to authentic stories.

The Student Empowerment Session (SES) qualifies for the Stickiness Factor and it is detailed in chapter 11. That session begins with the true account of a young girl named Kimberly Weisel who was taunted and ridiculed by her classmates in elementary school when she became bald because of chemotherapy treatments. Students are deeply touched by the taunting she experienced and the pain she felt, and always remember the "Kim Story."

At the end of a conversation, we tend to recall more of what we had to say than what others offered. When students actively participate in the lively SES discussion, the comments they make will stick with them but the most compelling part of the SES comes at the conclusion when many students are moved to apologize to classmates they have offended. Gladwell says that the Stickiness Factor has "to be memorable and move us to action."

The Power of Context

What are the details to which we must be attentive? The Power of Context is illustrated by the Mariner Middle School in Florida's Lee County School District. Statistics were collected on Violence Related Incidents (VRI) from the time the new school opened its doors in the fall of 2004. VRI include battery, disruption, disrespect, fighting, gang-related act, horseplay, insubordination, peer conflict, profanity, sexual harassment, threat/intimidation, and weapons possession. In the 2005–2006 school year, the student population jumped from 782 students to 1,292 students and the total VRI from 1,407 to 4,852. It is important to note that while the student population less than doubled, violence more than tripled.

Kathleen Saucier, a Certified BullySafeUSA Trainer, became the school counselor in the fall of 2006. She began conducting Student Empowerment Sessions, training the staff on bullying behaviors, working with parents and serving as a counseling resource to hundreds of students who were dealing with countless personal and family problems. She facilitated bullying-prevention activities, focusing on relationships and respect, and secured grants from the local Chamber of Commerce to purchase copies of Stephen Covey's *Seven Habits of Highly Effective Teens* (1998) for her students.

Saucier dressed as a clown, brought laughter into her presentations, told stories, and cajoled and confronted her students. Verbal bullying was treated as seriously as physical bullying. She activated and empowered students to have a voice in the legislative process as the state moved forward to pass antibullying legislation. She contributed information on the school website and submitted articles in the newsletter that went to parents. Through it all, she was relentless about paying attention to the important little infractions.

At the end of the 2006–2007 school year, the total student population had leveled off at 977 and the VRI dropped to 1,386. There was a significant drop in every category. The largest decrease was in the area of disruption, from 2,982 to 666. Insubordination was reduced from 689 to 180, profanity from 274 to 111 and peer conflicts fell from 209 to 100. The Broken Windows theory was put in play by enforcing rules against profanity, insubordination, and disruption, along with battery, fighting, and weapons possession. Simultaneously, positive behaviors were rewarded and recognized.

The complete statistical information chart from Mariner Middle School is shown in figure 9.1.There are three sets of data: 2004–2005, first year of school; 2005–2006, pre-intervention year; and 2006–2007 the postintervention year.

OFFENSE	SY0405	SY0506	SY0607
BAT	50	46	16
DIS	503	2982	666
DRS	381	192	117
FIT	58	141	62
GRA	0	9	5
HRS	82	243	110
INS	141	689	180
PRC	90	209	100
PRO	57	274	111
SXH	10	5	2
TRE	33	43	12
WPO	2	19	5
Total Incidents	1407	4852	1386
Total Student Pop	782	1292	977
BAT	Battery		
DIS	Disruption		
DRS	Disrespect		
FIT	Fighting		
GRA	Gang Related Act		
HRS	Horseplay		
INS	Insubordination		
PRC	Peer Conflict		
PRO	Profanity		
SXH	Sexual Harassment		
TRE	Threat/Intimidation		
WPO	Weapons Poss		

Figure 9.1

Peer and Community Influence

Judith Harris, author of *The Nurture Assumption* (1999), a rather controversial book, maintains that family influence is not always as important as we have been led to believe. She argues that peer influence and community influence are more significant in determining how children turn out. One of her most potent examples is that even when parents speak a foreign language at home, children are more inclined to use the language and accent of their peer group. Based on studies of juvenile delinquency and high-school drop-out rates, she posits that a child is better off in a good neighborhood and a troubled family than he or she is in a troubled neighborhood and a good family that supports Gladwell's Power of Context Concept. What outcomes can we expect of a child from a troubled family, living in a troubled neighborhood, attending a troubled school? How much influence can a good school have in spite of a troubled neighborhood where many troubled families live? Harris calls on us to keep our minds open to disturbing questions. We know there are many schools that serve as an anchor for children when their family life is turbulent. Certainly, the influence of peers needs to be included as we challenge our thinking.

CHANGING THE CULTURE

In our travels we have come across wonderful people, doing innovative thinking—people who are looking at the bigger picture and expanding their concerns from problem solving into grappling with systemic change. These visionaries are incubating approaches that might very well become institutionalized at some point in the future.

The White House Conference on Bullying Prevention that took place on March 10, 2011, gathered a diverse group of educators; parents; students; professionals; representatives of religious, racial, and gender minorities; and researchers. Several reccurring themes emerged from the day-long discussions—empower students; community involvement; more research; multiple approaches; continued concern for students at the college level; the impact of technology; and finding caring adults in every school. The compelling need to change the culture of meanness surfaced over and over—including a focus on prevention, not just punishment.

At the conference, national commitments to assist in changing the culture were made by the Parent Teachers Association and the National Education Association. The PTA launched an initiative to encourage PTAs across the country to lead conversations in their school communities about bullying. Planning tools and ideas for events have been disseminated through their national network.

The NEA released a rigorous, large-scale research study of its members through a representative sample of 5,064 NEA teachers and ESPs (education support professionals). Cyberbullying and sexting were identified as areas where all staff needed additional training. With regard to special populations, areas of greatest need for additional training related to sexual orientation, gender issues, and disability.

Positive Behavior Interventions and Support

Positive Behavior Interventions and Support (PBIS) is an exciting initiative that began at the University of Oregon many years ago. The program stresses teaching the behaviors you expect from students, the same as you would with academic concepts. PBIS is not a set program, but something that is created by the administrators and teachers within their building.

At Blackhawk Middle School in Bensenville, Illinois, the PBIS team also included students. The team met over the summer and looked at behavior concerns from the previous school year. From this came the creation of a matrix of behavioral expectations: Be Safe, Be Respectful, and Be Ready. These words are found throughout the school building—the halls, every classroom, and in every student's assignment notebook. Every teacher implemented the Behavior Lesson Plans that were designed by the PBIS team and discussed the desired behaviors to their students on the first day of classes. For example, under "Be Respectful," the behavior expectations include "Use positive and appropriate language" and "Be kind and polite to everyone." Reteaching and reminding continued throughout the year.

As opposed to traditional approaches that focus only on undesired behaviors, PBIS stresses a constant recognition of compliance with the behavioral expectations. Every six weeks a Celebration of Good Behavior takes place during lunch for students who have honored the matrix with a limited number of office referrals and no suspensions.

An additional incentive is Blackhawk Bucks that are passed out by teachers to students who demonstrate exceptional behavior. The reward for accumulating Blackhawk Bucks includes VIP seating at assemblies, going to the front of the lunch line for a week, and even lunch with a staff member of the student's choosing. Fried worked with every grade level the previous year, conducting Student Empowerment Sessions that focused on bullying reduction. In conjunction with the PBIS, if a student is bullying another student, a witness may say, "You're not using positive language" or "You're supposed to be kind and polite to everyone."

According to Nicole Robinson, Blackhawk Vice-Principal, in-school and out-of-school suspensions have dropped dramatically in the areas of bullying and fighting. When we are successful in dramatically reducing bullying, we need to fill the vacuum with a positive force. If we don't, physics informs us that the negative behavior will rush back in to fill the space. For more information about Positive Behavior Intervention and Support (PBIS) go to www.pbis.org.

Saturation Effect

Years ago, Jay Winsten, PhD, Director of the Center for Health Communication, Harvard School of Public Health, came up with the concept of the Designated Driver that has clearly changed the drinking and driving habits of millions of Americans. To accomplish that amazing change in social behavior, he orchestrated a "saturation effect" for Mothers Against Drunk Driving (MADD). There were national ad campaigns, articles in newspapers and journals, testimonials, and an easy-to-remember slogan—"Don't Drink and Drive." Winsten even persuaded writers of popular soap operas to use cocktail party scenes to script persons relinquishing their car keys when they had too much to drink. A wonderful example on the current scene is Chrissa, an American Girl "Girl of the Year" doll (2009). There is no better way to reach countless young girls than with a popular doll who finds the courage to stand strong and speak out about bullying.

When Fried was a practicing dance therapist at several psychiatric hospitals in the Kansas City, Missouri, area, she learned a valuable lesson from a patient, Brent, who had been an advertising executive prior to admitting himself for therapy. One morning, the movement therapy session focused on the subject of change. At the conclusion of the session, the group was discussing resistance to change, even when change is highly desired. As we pondered the contradiction, Brent offered to share something he had learned in "advertising school." He told us that marketing experts had done elaborate research to discover that it takes twenty-one contacts to convince a consumer to change their soap powder. If it takes twenty-one contacts to change attitudes about a product, imagine how many contacts are required to change an ingrained behavior.

Replacing Bullying with Kindness

The Saturation Effect is exactly what Mary Jane Cole and her staff created at Roosevelt Elementary School in Park Ridge, Illinois. Mary Jane Cole, former principal, invited Fried to work with their students, staff, and parents. The next year, Fried returned to conduct a BullySafeUSA Train the Trainer Institute for counselors and other staff members from all of the elementary and middle schools in the Park Ridge-Niles School District. The Institute was sponsored by the Emotional Learning Foundation (ELF), a group of community citizens who raise money to support innovative school projects throughout the school district.

An outgrowth of that was the development of a Kindness Activities Program by staff from the Roosevelt Elementary School who participated in the Training Institute. They pulled together activities from a curriculum guide, "30 Activities for Getting Better at Getting Along," by Fried and Lang (2005) from the magazine *Teaching Tolerance*, a publication of the Southern Poverty Law Center; a selected book list to support the activities developed by the teachers; a collection of kindness songs contributed by the school music teacher; and a community service project where the Student Council raised five thousand dollars, matched by the PTO, for Operation Smile, a program that provides surgeries for children with cleft palates.

The students are introduced on a daily basis to positive messages of kindness and compassion, coming to them in a variety of engaging ways. Cole says: "One thing to remember is that this district has an initiative to educate the whole child, not just preparing them for high test scores but preparing them to develop into caring and compassionate people."

Another kindness program that uses saturation was developed by a school counselor, Jacque DeJesus, in the Blue Valley School District in Shawnee Mission, Kansas. When you walk through the front door of his school, you enter a magical kingdom of kindness. There are pictures of students with their essays on kindness. There are paper chains with the names of students who have performed an act of kindness for someone in the school. There are drawings and posters with kindness sayings everywhere your eyes can take you.

Once a year, a contest is held and every student writes an essay about his/her Kindest Kansas Citizen. Family members are not eligible. Each class selects a winning essay and the Kindest Kansas Citizens who were described are invited to attend a school assembly to listen to the essay, read aloud by the student. The honored citizens have been teachers, neighbors, coaches, the school crossing guard, a physician, a soldier, and the school custodian, among others. Tears of joy reign! Every student essay that is written is mailed to the honored person. What a glorious surprise to open the mail and discover that a student wrote an essay about you!

Another activity that leaped from the classroom to the adult world began when DeJesus presented a Kindness Seminar to all of the teachers in her building. Upon their return to their classrooms they were requested to speak to their students about kindness to each other, their parents, their siblings, their pets, and their environment and talk to them about how they felt when someone was kind to them and how they felt when they were kind to someone else.

Following that discussion, DeJesus instructed the teachers to be alert to a spontaneous act of kindness that a student performed. At such a moment, the teacher would place a special object, such as a red wooden apple, on the student's desk as a way of acknowledging that student's act of kindness. The student was then instructed to watch for another student's kind act and transfer the apple to that student's desk.

What followed was remarkable! Teachers reported that students started overdosing on kindness because they wanted the apple on their desk. One teacher even recounted the day a boy dropped his pencil and four students dove to the floor to return it to its owner. The culture in the classrooms and the entire school changed.

When a group of us in the community, including Fried and Sosland, learned of this project, we decided that adults could benefit from this serial idea of kindness recognition. We wear buttons that say: "Kindness Is Contagious, Catch It!" (created by artist Rita Blitt) or "Power of Kindness" (created by philanthropist Norman Polsky) and pass them on to someone we witness performing an act of kindness. It is very fulfilling to be able to honor such genuine gifts of the human spirit and we are always pleased by how meaningful it is to the person when we pass the button forward.

The Art of Creating Change

The status quo has tremendous advantage because "it exists, therefore it is." It has a history and it has advocates for its perpetuity. To alter the status quo we must first question current tenets, build support for their removal, and then have a compelling replacement plan at hand.

A crisis can be a boon to promote change. People are more willing to question existing norms and take risks for change if a series of problems have surfaced. Fred Pryor, of Fred Pryor Seminars says that, "We are more inclined to risk the pain of change when the pain of staying the same is greater." We defined the crisis and the pain in chapter 1, when we identified health issues, truancy and drop-out data, increase in youth suicides and crime, teacher shortages, and learning deficits.

Increasing support for changing practices is coming from an awesome collection of people who are giving visibility and support for reexamining school practices. Home schooling and admissions to parochial and private schools are on the rise, giving additional evidence to the clamor for change.

Arne Duncan, who was appointed Secretary of Education by President Barack Obama in 2009, has a vision for a radical change in our educational system. During a television interview with Charlie Rose, he spoke of schools being open from 9:00am to 9:00pm, seven days a week, 52 weeks a year. The schools would function from 9-3, and nonprofit groups would take over from 3-9, offering a full complement of after school programs, including drama, debate, chess, tutoring, sports, and mentoring. Literacy programs would be offered for adults, as well as GED courses.

He went on to share that every school has a library, a gym, and computer labs, which could be used by the community. Health services, including dental services, could be brought into the school environment, which would essentially become a Community Center. Duncan argues that society has changed and schools haven't caught up with the new norm that requires "a different mindset."

A new mindset doesn't always start with educators. In the early 1990s, Bert Berkley, a Kansas City, Missouri, business leader, was asked by the Missouri Secretary of the Division of Family Services, Gary Stangler, to bring a business approach to the delivery of social services. The result was a citizen-based reform organization, named the Local Investment Commission (LINC).

As the group set about designing a one-stop resource base for children and families, they realized that schools were the logical setting. The group slowly began establishing what it called Caring Communities Sites in schools throughout the metropolitan area. Health, dental, and social services came together under one roof. An enlightened Before and After School concept began in one school and grew to seventy-five within six years. The core value of the Caring Community Site is that local citizens must come together and design a plan that meets their neighborhood needs. LINC then helps make it happen! To learn more about LINC, go to www.kclinc.org.

The time is ripe for a different mindset, new thinking, and creative energy to change our culture. Our country is going through a cultural, moral, and financial tsunami and a lot of people are in pain. What a perfect time to become a community of change agents!

Through countless contacts, connections, and conversations with passionate people who don't work in schools because it's a job, but because they want to use their lives in the service of children and our future, we have collected a list of ideas that speak to creating a culture of caring. No single idea is a guarantee for change. It will require a combination of many concepts, a collaboration of many people to be the equivalent of installing a sewer system and it will require individual change agents to become champions for the dream.

As you read the ideas for our change agents in the next chapter, we hope you will be inspired to put as many ideas as feasible in place, to add your own ingenuity and to create a "Tipping Point."

10

Change Agents

"Be the change that you wish to see in the world."

—Mohandas Gandhi

This chapter provides a multitude of ideas from a multitude of sources. The Change Agents are listed under the titles of people best positioned to carry them out, not in any necessary order. Originally parents were included as part of the Change Agents, but instead, a whole chapter has been devoted to their important role.

SCHOOL PRINCIPAL/ADMINISTRATORS

The principal sets the tone for the entire school and is the most significant Change Agent. The values of the principal will influence every decision and can lift a school to extraordinary heights or condemn a school to a political battlefield.

Stake out your commitment to affect the culture of your school and to involve every single adult who has a presence in your building. Share your goal to engage students and parents in this exciting enterprise and appoint a Task Force to develop a comprehensive plan. Bulliers can be monitored and converted. Targets can be supported and empowered. Witnesses can play a pivotal role in maneuvering power issues.

Staff training on effective bullying prevention and intervention techniques is a must. Having a shared vision by the administration, faculty and nonteaching staff is the foundation for a school-wide approach. Make a special effort to receive input from cafeteria workers, custodians, bus drivers, and all other adults who have contact with students. They have extensive information about student behavior that is untapped.

Measure the success of your effort with a pretest and posttest instrument. The Mariner Middle School Instrument in chapter nine is an example. Conduct a survey to capture attitudes and observations about peer behavior. The following three examples were created and used by Kathleen Saucier, a Certified BullySafeUSA Trainer:

Survey Statement: Students my age should not tease in a mean way, or spread unkind rumors about other students.

Survey Result: 94.23 percent of students won't gossip about their classmates because spreading rumors is not cool!

Survey Statement: Students should not shove, kick, hit, hair pull, or trip another student.

Survey Result: 96.23 percent of students won't physically bully other students because they have better things to do!

Survey Statement: Students should always try to be friendly with students who are different from them.

Survey Result: 92.92 percent of students believe it is the right thing to do to be friendly with someone who is different from them.

Students were pleased to learn that they were part of a large majority of students who were thinking positively. The survey results instilled a sense of pride in their school.

Define bullying as part of the school Code of Conduct. We recommend that physical, verbal, emotional, gender/sexual, and cyberbullying be specifically spelled out as unacceptable behaviors. Some schools have delineated very detailed rules and consequences for offenses. The more complicated the codes are, however, the less likely they are to be remembered. Principal Phil Hackett, of the Edwin Green Elementary School in Cincinnati, Ohio, has had great success with the following conduct code: "Respect Yourself, Respect Others, Respect the Environment." The code is easy for everyone to memorize and all inappropriate behaviors fit into one of those commandments. Of course, all behaviors are closely monitored and enforced.

Many antibullying speakers, curriculum, and programs have proven their usefulness.

Even the most powerful speaker requires follow-through and continuous reinforcement. Many schools will bring in a presentation as a kick-off to a year-long comprehensive commitment.

Make a very strong statement about your core beliefs at the entrance to your school.

Hang pictures of heroes accompanied by their memorable sayings in the front hall. Posters and student art that are substantive as well as decorative can be strong visual behavior reminders. The constant presence of these eye-catching prompts has an amazing capacity to affect students' attitudes.

Tap into Character Education programs that highlight a significant Word of the Month. The program is a process rather than a curriculum, and many schools have developed exciting ways to bring the Word of the Month to life.

Use chants, affirmations, and/or verbal rituals to begin each school day. At the Forrest Elementary School in Hampton, Virginia, Principal Kimberly Garvin-Richardson begins the day with her students reciting a creed:

> I WILL show respect to others, property, and myself
> I WILL accept responsibility for my actions
> I WILL listen to and follow directions
> I WILL use appropriate language
> I WILL do my best at all times.

Give playground supervision and recess options a high priority. Recess is one of the most frequently mentioned hot spots for bullying. When teachers are assigned to playground duty, it is essential that they spread themselves out and not cluster together. Playground supervisors and parent volunteers can make a tremendous difference. In spite of the concerns, recess has important benefits. Sacrificing play and downtime for more test preparation is not productive.

New research suggests that recess can influence behavior, concentration, and even grades. Romina M. Barros, a pediatrician and the lead researcher of a study on this topic published in 2009 claims that: "We should understand that kids need that break because the brain needs that break." In their study of eleven thousand eight- and nine-year-old children, they found that those who had more than fifteen minutes of recess a day showed better behavior in class than those who had little or none. Physical activity is especially important for young males.

In middle and high schools, insist that teachers stand in the halls between classrooms. Crowded hallways are ripe for cruelty. Awareness and supervision can make a tremendous difference for students at risk.

Cafeterias are another hot spot for bullying where supervision is required. Some principals take on the lunchroom duties so their teachers can have that precious time to be with their colleagues or have time for themselves.

Uniforms or some kind of uniform dress code are becoming more and more popular. Clothing issues, especially for girls, can be a horrendous source of taunting. Fashion trends, especially when students come from diverse economic backgrounds, can cause problems. Dress codes, such as solid color pants and white shirts, can defuse a lot of issues. This type of uniform can instill a sense of pride while limiting ridicule. It can also cut through the complicated codes and enforcement of how short a skirt or shorts should be, or the difference between narrow blouse straps or spaghetti straps. Many students have confided that they complained bitterly about the rule but were secretly thrilled to be relieved of the clothing competition.

Social and emotional learning for students have proven their worth. Programs that give children life-skill training to make wise choices, sensible decisions, and function ethically not only turn out students who are good citizens, they increase academic achievement. An amazing study by Roger P. Weissberg and Joseph Durlak analyzed over three hundred research studies and concluded that when social and emotional learning programs were offered, students ranked at least ten percentile points higher than their counterparts who were not involved in such programs. They also had better attendance records, were often less disruptive, and were less likely to be suspended.

Appreciate that bulliers, especially at the elementary-school level, are students with problems. Discipline must be enforced, but getting to the root of acting-out behavior is equally important. Every child needs at least one person who believes in him or her. When a parent is not that believer, someone else must step up to the role.

Stress witness training for students. Many school tragedies have been thwarted because student witnesses were privy to plans, threats, or bullying that they reported to authorities. Emphasize the importance of reporting information in confidence for the safety of everyone in school.

If possible, have an Open Door policy. A middle-school principal in Baltimore announced that a jar of hard candies was on his desk and students were always welcome to come to his office, obtain a piece of candy, and stay for a brief visit. This was meant to encourage students to feel free to come to his office without being suspected of tattling or having gotten in trouble. This is especially important to increase reports by witnesses of bullying behavior.

Encourage community service and volunteer activities. There are so many ways students can begin to contribute and feel part of their community. Students who feel a sense of belonging and purpose are less likely to seek revenge for hurts. They are learning to make a connection between their community service and life experience.

Don't pay special deference to athletes at the high-school level. Sports "stars" need to adhere to the same rules and consequences as all other students. It is tragic to realize how many of our professional hero athletes have become corrupted and destroyed by the fame they couldn't handle.

Sexual language about gender orientation is rampant in middle and high schools. Confront the subject directly and reiterate that every child deserves to be safe in school—safe from physical, verbal, emotional, sexual, and cyberbullying attacks. When you describe how infractions will be handled, be sure to enforce the described discipline the first time one occurs—and every time thereafter.

Once you embark on a school-wide bullying prevention plan, all teachers must spell out the expectations and be consistent in dealing with infractions. If some educators follow the accepted plan and others don't, students will learn how to work the system and take advantage of any leniency.

Include art experiences—visual arts, plays, songs, dances, and musical productions.

Proponents for Creative Expression programs cite numerous studies showing the value of arts in academic performance, sticking with tasks, school attendance, participation in math and science fairs, fewer court referrals, and better attitudes. For high-school students, there is both a play and a video titled: "Bang, Bang, You're Dead." It is incredibly powerful when performed by the high-school drama department, and the video is extremely effective.

To change the culture will require the equivalent of a three-legged stool—the school, the students, and the parents. Inform all parents of your intentions to create a safe, caring, compassionate environment. Ask your PTA or PTO organization to host a meeting on the subject of school safety that includes a number of incentives—such as a spaghetti dinner, free babysitting services, and a "No-Homework" night. Use older students to help with babysitting and serving. Do not announce the meeting as a Bullying Program. Parents of the bulliers and the witnesses will not attend and parents of the targets will attend with expectations of personal solutions. For those who do not attend, distribute a newsletter that outlines your plans, and emphasize the vocabulary you will be using and the school Code of Conduct. Create a Power Point presentation about your concerns, your goals, your activities, and some early successes. Make presentations to your local Chamber of Commerce, civic groups, and business leaders. Engage them and request contributions to fund specific aspects of your program—speakers, trainings, books, films, incentives, and so on. Contact your local newspaper to document your year-long program.

VICE-PRINCIPALS

Many principals are fortunate to have vice-principals. Vice-principals are frequently assigned to deal with student behavior issues. The discipline style you adopt will carry a strong message in the school environment. It is very important to hold students accountable and administer appropriate consequences while maintaining a connection to the young person, if possible. A business executive donated a badly needed gymnasium to his former high school in honor of an administrator who never gave up on him. When he became successful he found a way to thank his disciplinarian/mentor for believing in him at his most unlovable stage.

Stay current with the latest research. Empathy training is becoming more popular, not only in education circles but in medical schools. Reports of mirror neuron research provide hard data about the ability of people to feel what others are feeling. When you can substantiate suggestions with evidenced-based research, you will be given more opportunities to try your ideas. If your principal dismisses requests for bullying programs or projects because he or she is on overload, be an enthusiastic advocate and take responsibility for bringing such valuable activities into the school. Keep a daily journal about your experience as a vice-principal. Observe your principal's strengths and weaknesses, successes and failures with an open mind and be grateful for the training opportunity.

CLASSROOM TEACHERS

In some cases, teachers can be an even greater influence than parents in a student's world. You may never receive the gratitude you deserve, but never doubt the power you have to change a life.

Institute classroom meetings every morning or several mornings a week at the elementary level. Creative teachers have put all kinds of special rituals in practice to ground students for the day, to instill manners and social etiquette, to resolve conflicts, and to teach children the art of giving and receiving compliments.

Many middle schools have daily Home Room meetings that can be used effectively to deal with peer relationship and behavior issues. If you are a Home Room teacher, especially for first-year students, your classroom may be the very best opportunity to establish a trusting atmosphere where students can feel free to express the challenges of the middle-school transition.

Humor is a winner! When students are asked to identify their favorite teacher, at any grade level, invariably it is someone who brings laughter to the classroom. If you tend to be on the serious side, consider the element of surprise and wear a clown nose one day, act out a lesson by changing your voice, throw in a joke or two, invite students to share a funny story, perform a magic trick to demonstrate a point. Be sure not to confuse humor with sarcasm.

Create a rap song to teach the multiplication tables or other problematic assignments. Tom McFadden, a Stanford University biology instructor, produced a rap video, "Regulatin' Genes" for his students that has received more than fifty thousand views on YouTube. Check it out!

Demand civility and courtesy and intervene immediately when inappropriate behaviors occur. Make this a priority at the beginning of the year and monitor consistently thereafter. Honor students who show respect, compassion, and kindness.

Include antibullying activities and exercises throughout the year. Changing behaviors and creating a sense of family requires constant reinforcement. Make your classroom a sanctuary of safety.

Teach your students the concept of empathy. It should be a part of every student's understanding and behavior repertoire, yet many students are unfamiliar with the term.

Use every opportunity to keep empathy alive and active with your classes. No bullying-prevention program can succeed without empathy practice.

At faculty meetings, add social and emotional learning skills to the academic agenda. Decide on a focus for the week, such as no put-downs, a particular character trait, intentional acts of kindness.

Share personal stories of recovering from mistakes, lessons learned, triumphing over difficult times. It is very meaningful to students to discover that teachers were on the receiving end of painful bullying experiences and channeled that experience into a teaching career.

Don't dismiss the quiet child who is not quick to raise his or her hand and participate in class discussions. The extroverted students will get lots of attention from other adults. Be the one person, perhaps, who recognizes the potential of someone who is often invisible to others but has a depth that hasn't been discovered.

Work at being fair and just with all of your students. It is normal to have preferences, but being "teacher's pet" can cause major problems for a favored child.

Do not make comparisons with a student's sibling, for better or worse. Brothers and sisters can have entirely different personalities, capacities, motivations, and experiences in their family.

Never humiliate or ridicule a student. Never allow a student to be humiliated or ridiculed in your class.

Encourage students to report bullying situations and experiences to you. Assure them of your confidentiality and your desire to protect them from being in jeopardy. Talk to them about the difference between tattling and reporting.

If you lose your temper and behave in a way that you regret, apologize. Students need to see adults who take responsibility for their errors. Many parents never apologize for their mistakes and young people can benefit enormously from hearing and seeing a sincere, adult apology.

When you witness a colleague who is bullying students, take some constructive action. You would not want your own child to be in the classroom of a bullying teacher for an entire school year.

Establish a working partnership with the parents of your students. Try to develop empathy for an especially difficult parent, or at least for that person's child. Dealing with parents of bulliers who are in denial is a special challenge. We will deal more thoroughly with this issue in future chapters.

Be sure to find ways to deal with your stress. Don't be too hard on yourself and take time to appreciate all that you give day after day after day.

If some of these ideas are of value to you, make a place for them in your lesson planning book so they will stay on your radar screen.

PHYSICAL EDUCATION INSTRUCTORS

Phys-ed or gym can be one of the most uncomfortable periods in the day for some students. Please do away with selecting captains and having them choose teams. Use a deck of cards to select teams or any other random, imaginative way you can think of. A parent comment: "The phys-ed instructors were always good at sports so they can't fathom what it's like to be picked last, time after time."

Check locker room behavior frequently. Keep students on their toes with your surprise visits. Do not allow hazing activities to become part of an athletic ritual. Too many students have suffered severe emotional and sometimes physical experiences because of hazing. Be adamant about your disapproval of such activity.

SPECIAL EDUCATION TEACHERS

Bless you! You have one of the most demanding roles in the educational system.

You have a special heart for children with special needs and you choose to share their survival journey.

However possible, find ways for your students to be treated with respect by their peer group. Work with the school nurse or the school counselor to make a special pitch about the difficulties that special-ed students struggle with to all of the other classes. Enlist a pledge from all students to be supportive at best, indifferent at worst but never to add additional burden to their daily challenges.

Discuss the different kinds of bullying that can occur and assure your students that they are not to blame when it happens. Talk about the best strategies to respond to their tormentors and have feedback sessions after they have tried out some of the ideas.

Have your students write some poems or essays about experiences they have with bullying situations that can be printed in the school newspaper. If there are some regular students who have been particularly helpful and kind, ask permission to include their names in the article.

Recruit some remarkable students to be a support group. Judy Bennet, an Inclusion Facilitator in the Shawnee Mission School District, organized a Circle of Friends for a special-ed student, Stephen Rouse, who has Down syndrome. She formed the group during their last year at elementary school to carry Stephen through the treacherous transition to middle school and the succeeding years. The group often met on weekends and after school. They went to movies, attended concerts, shared family vacations, and visited Stephen at his job. Stephen's parents were thrilled beyond measure when he graduated from high school with a B average and attended college away from home. Their appreciation for the Circle of Friends program is unbounded!

PARA-PROFESSIONALS

A para-professional is often an indispensable member of a school team. They are usually assigned to specific students to ensure that such students with special needs are being monitored. Many special-needs students are mainstreamed for most of the day and it is crucial for these students to have someone to keep them on task, to help them with reading problems, and to help the teacher handle any issues that that student is dealing with in the classroom.

Because of the nonjudgmental, personal support you offer, you serve as a trusted advocate for your charges. You make sure that special students don't fall through the cracks and get behind in their work. You constantly give the message that "You are capable! I will be there for you and you will succeed."

If you notice any of your students being bullied—add to your agenda a series of steps they can take to stop the hurtfulness. At the same time, because you believe in them, they can learn to believe in themselves and keep situations in perspective.

SCHOOL COUNSELORS, PSYCHOLOGISTS, SOCIAL WORKERS

You are an invaluable resource for your school principal because you have your finger on the pulse of the school. You have the unique capacity to be an advocate for students, for parents, for teachers and other staff, and for programs and concepts that you have researched.

Use your skills to lead class discussions on bullying prevention. Consider offering the Student Empowerment Session for all the classes in your school as outlined in chapter 11. Determine a method to measure and evaluate the effectiveness of your program.

Arrange for staff training on bullying prevention and intervention, including special education and para-educators. Be sure to make the training available to nonteaching staff as well, such as school nurses, cafeteria workers, custodians, bus drivers, playground supervisors, parent volunteers, school secretaries, media specialists, school resource officers, crossing guards, music and art teachers.

Put weekly memos in teachers' boxes with a bullying-prevention idea. Recruit the artistic students, who are often on the fringes and rebuffed, to add graphics to the memos or to create cartoons on the topic.

Provide counseling for students who bully and are bullied. Do not bring them together to resolve a conflict unless the target requests such a session. Most targets will not feel comfortable divulging the extent of their abuse in the presence of their abuser.

When it is obvious that a student requires more intensive counseling than you can provide, take all necessary steps to see that such a student is referred for mental healthcare.

Research curriculum, videos, programs, speakers, books, and any materials that are effective tools for individual and group sessions. Identify best practices.

Offer empathy training sessions for every classroom and with all students. Empathy training is essent for bullying prevention.

Organize peer helpers, peer mentors, and student-support programs. Talk with older students in the school about reaching out to younger students. In middle school, match up sixth graders with responsible eighth graders as they begin this new experience. Discuss the risks and consequences of hazing.

Female bullying is especially vicious. Address this subject with girls, at all age levels. Numerous resources on this topic are available via the Internet. Most important is a frank, forthright discussion, facilitated by a skilled leader, such as yourself.

Match up every student who moves into your school with a trustworthy "buddy." New students are overwhelmed, some are grieving for the loss of familiar surroundings, and they are often rejected and excluded. They deserve a special welcoming process.

Become an advocate for bullying intervention and prevention in your school. Use your acquired skills to be persuasive with administrators who don't recognize the extent or consequences of bullying. Be a support to teachers who want to emphasize bullying prevention.

Conduct parent sessions on antibullying. Meet informally with parents of each grade level and explain the school's concerns, policies, and programs. Be prepared to deal with personal issues.

An astute counselor at one high school recruited and trained the top athletes to volunteer at a children's hospital. They had been treated so deferentially by students and staff that they became very full of themselves. She saw hospital service, where their athletic achievements were unknown, as a means to give them a different perspective on their reality.

Keep tabs on antibullying legislation and use your connections with your professional networks to support or oppose bills under consideration.

SCHOOL NURSES

You may be the first adult in the system to become aware of a student who is a target.

Students who complain of stomachaches and headaches at recess time are giving signals of distress. Use their trust wisely when giving information to other staff.

At the beginning of the elementary school year, prepare a presentation on various health issues that students might be dealing with. In every classroom discuss hand washing, cancer, epilepsy, Tourette's, postsurgery recovery, diabetes, ADD and ADHD, allergies, Asperger's syndrome, vision problems, asthma, children with disabilities, special needs, and any other diseases and illnesses that need to be brought to their attention. Talk about medications that students might need to take, such as Ritalin, insulin, and so on, and how important it is not to make fun of someone on medication. Emphasize how fortunate students are who do not have to deal with health problems and how embarrassing and uncomfortable it is for students who are taunted because of matters they cannot control.

School nurses are frequently assigned to cover sexuality, puberty, and harassment. Become known as a resource in the system who is comfortable with this subject matter.

Have a private conversation with the parents of any students with health needs to see how you can be an advocate for their child in the system.

Share your knowledge and wisdom with administrators, counselors, and teachers.

Offer to be present at a parent conference with a teacher who needs support about a bullying situation.

BUS DRIVERS, CAFETERIA WORKERS, AND CUSTODIANS

Request an opportunity to be involved in any antibullying training sessions that take place.

Insist that students treat you with respect and courtesy. Request that such courtesy become part of the Student Code of Conduct. Appreciate the special observations and information you have to offer.

Reach out to students whom you recognize are suffering. Because of your special role, you have unusual opportunities to offer support and caring.

Bus drivers have an awesome responsibility to maintain safety and order simultaneously. There are always some students who will take advantage of this dual role. Student passenger behavior can include shouting, tripping, screaming obscenities, throwing spitballs, shoving students against windows, terrorizing younger children, destroying homework, and sexual harassment. Do not allow bullying behavior of any kind on your bus and make sure that you have the authority to expel disobedient students. More and more schools are installing surveillance cameras on school busses.

Ask for a specific staff liaison to receive reports of behavior issues, to receive information you overhear, and to deal with your concerns. When you make a report, ask to receive notification of any action taken. Suggest that all bus drivers meet on some regular basis with the staff liaison to provide feedback on bus behavior situations. When reports are made, become informed about any action taken.

When appropriate bus behavior becomes the norm at the very beginning of elementary school, it can prevent serious problems at the secondary level. When students are not responsive to rules, some bus drivers return to the school grounds until order prevails.

You are the first and the last contact of the school day. Use your twice-a-day connection to build a personal relationship with your passengers and their parents. Invite parents to come to the bus stop at the beginning of the year to become personally acquainted. A school district in Cincinnati has an Open House at the bus depot before school begins. Parents and children are invited to attend and "Get to Know Your Bus Driver."

Some bus drivers discover the birthdays of every student on their bus route and create a birthday ritual. Do something special for students with summer birthdays.

Cafeteria workers can spot children with eating disorders and students who are caught in food and lunch-money extortion. Share your valuable information with a staff liaison and ask to receive a report on action taken. A cafeteria worker observed a young girl who was only ordering a drink at lunch every day, reported it, and a case of anorexia was brought to attention.

Students on the free-lunch program may need some extra tender loving care on a Monday morning after a rough weekend at home. Hugs and extra helpings of cinnamon rolls can feed famished souls as well as empty tummies. Cafeteria personnel can set the tone for the beginning of a new week. Food-service staff have been known to offer a "job" to lonely students who are dropped off at school very early.

Custodians see students from a slightly different angle. They are more likely to come in contact with students in the hallways, the cafeteria, locker rooms, and bathrooms. They have rescued students who get locked in their lockers and have been known to clean bathrooms when they know that bulliers are going to enter the premises.

Request a staff liaison to work with you regarding behavior information about students. Mopping floors, with your supervision, is a more effective punishment than suspensions for students who relish the freedom from school.

Use your role to protect targets whenever possible. Bathrooms can be very dangerous places. Remove vulgar statements scrawled on bathroom walls as soon as possible and protect students from swirleys. Be on the look out for students with wet hair.

Locker rooms are another site of torment and vandalism where custodians can be watchful and intervene effectively.

In conversations with countless bus drivers, cafeteria workers, and custodians, we have found them to be caring people who consistently reach out to kids with problems. Their skills, their observations, and their good hearts deserve appreciation and respect.

MULTIMEDIA CENTER SPECIALISTS

Use your access to the Internet to identify resources that address peer cruelty, promote empathy, and inspire kindness for faculty and students.

Present a list of books for the PTA or PTO to purchase on the subject of bullying, stereotypes, and racism for different age levels, genders, and cultures.

Organize a special table to display books on bullying subjects. Invite students to write reviews about books they read with specific recommendations for age and gender and to rate the books from one to four stars. Post several reviews for each book that is read.

At the end of the year, publish a list of the books with the most stars and recommendations they have received.

Make arrangements to have older students read books about bullying problems to younger students. Especially invite bulliers to be readers. As the saying goes, "We learn by teaching."

Have students create unique bookmarks about bullying prevention. A student at Stephen Mack Middle School in Rockford, Illinois, came up with one that had the words STOP Problems, Anger, Insults, and Negativity (P A I N) on one side and BE Knowledgeable, Inclusive, Nicer, and Decent (K I N D) on the other.

MUSIC AND ART TEACHERS

Music and art instructors bring a special touch to the development of the whole child. A study that followed some twenty-five thousand students in one thousand schools across the United States discovered that students who were involved in arts programs showed higher academic performance, increased standardized test scores, lower drop-out rates, fewer court referrals, an increased ability to express anger appropriately, and were three times more likely to win an award for school attendance, among other positive findings.

Use your art and music background to encourage empathy and kindness. A Kindness Song is attached to the end of this chapter.

PLAYGROUND SUPERVISORS

Because the playground is one of the most terrorizing haunts for bulliers, it calls for unusual attention. Playground supervisors and the parent volunteers they supervise can make a tremendous difference. In addition to the overt expressions of physical and verbal abuse, playgrounds teem with examples of isolation and ostracizing.

One solution in use is a "Conversation Bench." An adult stands at the bench with a flag announcing that conversation is available. This is a great alternative for students who are often excluded or attacked during recess, without fear of being stigmatized. It is also beneficial for students with injuries and health issues.

A combination of unstructured and structured recess activities gives students a choice and relieves some of their concerns. Create a structured activity when you notice a number of children who are spending recess alone.

At Brooks Elementary School in Windsor, California, the PTA has arranged for an alternative recess. Every Friday, parent volunteers offer board games, bingo, bead-stringing projects, knitting, and arts and crafts in a room set aside for this purpose. They thought their project would attract a small group of children, but out of 450 students who share recess, 125 flock to the Activity Room and they have asked for the program to be extended to three days a week.

At Tillman Elementary School in Kirkwood, Missouri, they have two big rocks at the back of their playground that are used effectively to settle disputes. When a conflict occurs, students are directed to go to the Talking Rocks and "talk it out." A "Talking Tree" could work or some other playground landmark. Also at Tillman, Debbie Fechter, a staff member, takes photos of students who make good choices on the playground and other hot spot areas. Enlarged pictures of their smiling faces are displayed on the walls of the cafeteria all year.

SECRETARIES

Secretaries are the heart of Operation Central. Everything that happens in school radiates from the front office and defines the atmosphere of the school.

One of the most important roles is to serve as a buffer for the principal and vice-principal(s). Secretaries can defuse angry parents by taking information and presenting it to the administrators before the call is returned.

Become familiar with custody issues to make sure that a parent who is not the legal guardian does not remove a child from school.

Be the cheerful spirit in the office who sets a warm, inviting tone for all who enter. Treat students who are sent to the office for discipline with respect.

Request a "petty cash fund" for students who forget to bring lunch money, field trip money, and so on.

Never underestimate your capacity to be the "face" of the school and affect the school environment.

SCHOOL RESOURCE OFFICERS

SROs serve as educators, role models, youth advocates, a law enforcement presence, and a liaison with the community. They have wide latitude to listen and respond to children's needs, to deal with situations in a calm and effective manner, and offer security.

Take on bullying prevention and intervention as a high priority and offer to speak at parent and staff meetings. Inform students and parents about bullying behaviors that violate the law and how they can be charged and prosecuted.

Use your status to encourage exemplary behavior. Deputy Scott Thirkell, an SRO at an elementary school in Salina, Kansas, started a special program that recognizes students who have shown good citizenship, courtesy, kindness, and respect for others. Every two weeks, students are nominated by their classroom teachers to be a part of "Officer Scott's Lunch Bunch." They are seated at a table with a tablecloth and a special dessert. They also receive a certificate and an enlarged picture of their lunch group.

School crossing guards, along with bus drivers, are the first and last contact of the school day for those children who walk to school. We have heard heartwarming stories about these wonderful men and women who use their role to make personal connections with students. Being greeted with a smile and a wave that you can count on every day can smooth some rough edges—coming and going. Every adult contact has the potential to lift the spirit of a hurting child.

STUDENT ENGAGEMENT—WITH ADULT SUPPORT

Since students represent all three categories of bullying—bulliers, targets, and witnesses—no prevention program can succeed without involving students directly in the implementation of a plan. Children, as with adults, want to be able to control their circumstances. Knowledge is power. Engaging students in the solution of concerns is a very effective course of action.

Never underestimate the wisdom that will come from involving them in conversations and discussions. Young people know better than the rest of us how high the cost of bullying is. They need to understand that it is within their power to reduce the toll.

The Student Empowerment Session (see chapter 11) goes right to the core of student engagement. One counselor describes it as a "cleansing experience for the kids." Because it is presented in a generic way, it is nonthreatening. It is introduced as a teaching technique whereby students are educating adults about the breadth and depth of bullying. Students take the assignment seriously and it serves a double purpose, enlightening themselves and each other and educating adults. It is an extraordinary way to motivate students to become involved.

Witness training for all students is highly recommended. The adult community will never be in a position to observe all of the bullying activities that transpire. Witnesses need to feel empowered, confident, and safe to take some course of action. Witness training includes an understanding of the various ways that witnesses react to bullying scenes and options for constructive involvement. An activity that is part of the Student Empowerment Session (chapter 11) gives students a chance to consider high-risk versus low-risk interventions. The activity also plants the seed for greater courage once they embark on the path to be a responsible witness.

An extensive array of peer-mentoring and peer-support programs exist. They operate under many different names, such as Peer Mentors, Playground Pals, Befrienders, Buddies, Natural Helpers, and Peer Helpers, and have different priorities that include tutoring, emotional support, social inclusion, and other goals. One constant is that the quality of the training and the supervision determines the effectiveness. Another universal element is the need to recruit a wide range of student leadership, not just the top of the ladder group. If gangs are a problem at your school, include some gang leaders.

Restorative justice is a fairly new concept that has a number of advantages over punishment and expulsion. James Wilson, author of *The Moral Sense* (1995), looks at Three Reasons People Behave: Level One—To avoid pain; Level Two—For respect or reward from one another; Level Three—For respect of self. Diane Gossen, author of *It's All about WE, Rethinking Discipline Using Restitution* (2008), focuses on the latter. Instead of asking "Why didn't you do what you should have done?" Gossen asks: "How are you going to make things better?" "What's your plan to solve the problem?" "What kind of person do you want to be?" A preferable resolution for peer conflicts is for the bulliers to redeem themselves through mutually agreed upon restitution.

Students are never too young to learn the value of giving to others. All students can benefit from making a contribution to their community. Volunteerism has proven to reduce the school drop-out rate and to change the way young people feel about themselves, and it changes the way others see them.

Ron Poplau, a sociology instructor at Shawnee Mission Northwest High School in Kansas, created a community service credit course for high-school students. Over three hundred students work in the community, interact with senior citizens and younger children, and raise funds for worthy causes. In neighboring Missouri, via an alternative program, high-school students believe in "giving back." Students of Amy Seymour at the Main Street Academy shovel snow and work gardens for the elderly and reach out to disadvantaged children. They are learning to make a connection between their community-service projects and life experience.

Appreciation for diversity is essential in today's cosmopolitan atmosphere. Students of all races, cultures, religions, and gender differences are sharing neighborhoods, sports activities, and classrooms. Schools are the perfect forum to transcend prejudices that might come from the home or the community. Teaching Tolerance, a publication of the Southern Poverty Law Center, is, once again, a rich source of materials and ideas on this topic for use in the classroom.

In many schools, students of different races sit separately in the cafeteria. There are other divisions in the cafeteria that perpetuate student alienation. Sponsor a Mix-It-Up at Lunch Day once a month and spread the word that students are to sit at different tables, with different students than they usually join for lunch. Train some student leaders to facilitate a conversation and/or have young people sit at tables of their Birthday Month. Print out signs with the popular astrological qualities to encourage discussion.

Organize a panel of students with different cultural backgrounds to speak to social studies classes at the middle- and high-school level. Panel members should prepare a five-minute presentation and be prepared for a Question-and-Answer period to follow. Such a program was created by Farheen Haider when she was a Muslim student at Pascack Valley High School in New Jersey. She transformed her bullying experience into the creation of Origins—a multi-cultural panel of high school students who shared personal stories—to raise awareness about individual bias specific to cultural differences. She also set up a support group for Muslim students who were being targeted.

Using art and drama classes, engage students in designing antibullying and positive-behavior posters and performing skits that illustrate typical disrespectful behaviors with a revision on the rerun. Integrating the skits with willing teachers in the role of the bulliers can have a "stickiness" factor, especially when the bulliers get their "comeuppance."

Appoint a student Task Force on Cyberbullying at the middle- and high-school levels. The agenda could include the publication of a researched article in the school newspaper, a student definition of cyberbullying to be included in the Code of Conduct, a Student's Bill of Rights regarding freedom from cyberbullying, presentations to the state legislature regarding protection of students from cyberbullying, a cyberbullying pledge to be signed by all students, and any other ideas that develop from the Task Force.

Many schools have instituted a box where students can deposit anonymous tips about bullying that is happening to themselves or others. Place a box where students can nominate Champions of Change right next to the Tips Box, so if a student is seen approaching the boxes, it would be hard to determine his or her intent. The box needs to be secured to guarantee confidentiality. The designated adult who is assigned to deal with the Tips and the Champs must handle the situations with discretion. An Anonymous Tips Phone Line can be installed, in addition or instead. The rules governing the Tips Box, the Champions Box, and the Tips Line should be clearly explained to all students. Honor the Champions of Change who are nominated by their peers.

Call together a group of trustworthy students, ask for volunteers, and invite Champions of Change to become members of a team to create a social norm of kindness and compassion in your school. Explain the Law of the Few and the power of even a few students to make a noticeable change in the school environment. Ask them to create opportunities for inclusion for students who have been rejected. One creative example of this strategy was a high school Prom Queen who invited a male student to dance with her at the Prom. His status as an isolate was reversed and he claimed it was life-changing.

COMMUNITY

Every citizen is part of an energy imprint in our society. When a lot of angry people dump their hostility into a community, it infects our atmosphere. When people are intentionally kind and compassionate, something amazing can happen.

Much too often, young people are dismissed and disregarded by elders as troublesome. What would it take for all adults to look every child in the eye, smile, and greet them favorably, whenever they come in contact? What if we used our tone of voice and our body language to send out messages of respect for people of all ages?

Change Agents even work in prison. Members of an inmate self-help program, Reaching Out from Within, in seven Kansas correctional facilities, meet weekly and recite a pledge of nonviolence. They work on managing their anger and treat their fellow convicts with respect. Their calmer behavior has an effect on others and the recidivism rate for the Reaching Out from Within members averages 20.4 percent as compared to a national recidivism rate of between 50 and 67 percent.

"Dissing" is an underlying cause of a great deal of violence. A contest for a catchy slogan could be held. For example, "When I get dissed, I use my fist. When I'm respected, I act as expected."

An awesome example of a community Change Agent is Sue Head, Executive Director, Keeter Center for Character Education at College of the Ozarks, Branson, Missouri. Sue was asked by the Chancellor of her college to put a major emphasis on character. She took that one-sentence assignment and initiated an extraordinary journey for her community. She began with the belief that people really want to be engaged, they want to make the culture safer, fairer, better for everyone but are conditioned to wait for someone else to take responsibility.

Information had been released about the high rate of discipline issues in the schools. The first reaction from the community was to demand that the school administration do something about the problem! Sue's reaction was that teachers and the administration are being expected to do the impossible. "We are on the same team," she said. "We can't put another rock in the backpack of another teacher to climb a very steep hill!" Sue felt that students needed to be getting the message about their behavior from *everyone*—the YMCA, the dentist, McDonald's, the bus driver, at home, at Sunday schools. She reasoned that nobody cares as much about our community as we do, and when we link arms together, that is our greatest strength.

Coincidentally, she attended a Character Plus Conference and heard Joan Davis speak about the Character Education concept where the community gets to decide the traits they want to embrace. Sue had been looking for a tangible way to get everyone involved.

She returned to Branson and invited anyone who would listen to her to become a First PLACE Partner. PLACE stood for Partners Linking Arms for Character Education. It didn't cost any money, there was no product to buy, the requirement to be a partner was to sign up and give contact information. She met with every organization, agency, and individual she could find and ended up with one thousand names in a database.

The Character Education project recommended that the community be brought together to choose a "Word of the Month" that would promote good character. A Town Hall meeting was held to select the words. Attendees ranged from high-school students to retirees. Fifteen character traits were placed on a ballot and the assembled group could vote for nine words—one for each month of the school year. People came to the microphone and passionately defended the word they felt best represented their community.

The outcome was September—Respect, October—Responsibility, November—Citizenship, December—Compassion, January—Commitment, February—Honesty, April—Perseverance, May—Self-Discipline. Each word had a connection to a particular month. By the end of the evening, the people decided they wanted to continue during the summer so they added June—Patience, July—Patriotism, and August—Courage.

She sent word out to everyone in her database to find a way to be *intentional* about demonstrating the trait of the month. The results were astounding! A local construction company painted the words: Get Mixed Up with First PLACE in big black letters on the side of their yellow concrete mixing truck. Realtors created yard signs with the trait of the month. The word was printed on McDonald's receipts, utility bills, and bank teller's windows. The local newspaper ran a full page in color every month, listing all of the First PLACE Partners. The list grew to 550! A radio station featured a different school every month with the activities they were doing to celebrate the designated word.

Sue would deny that she is a Change Agent. She believes that the community was waiting for a catalyst to energize their spirit and that *every* community is poised to do the same. Branson discovered that when character becomes imbedded in the community culture and reinforced in the schools, more teaching goes on, math scores go up, and attendance increases. The ultimate testimonial came from a school administrator who reported that his disciplinary rate was down as much as 50 percent. The goal had come full circle.

Sue reports that the community went on to tackle even greater challenges. When the economic crisis devastated Branson's tourism industry and so many people lost their jobs, teachers were sending food home with students in their backpacks to get them through the weekend. The community is still linking arms to solve problems, this time dealing with poverty and hunger. At another Town Hall meeting, 1,400 volunteers served eight thousand people for dinner for seventy days—and the response continues as this is being written.

POLICY MAKERS

Forty-five states have passed antibullying legislation as of this writing. Check to see if your state has such a law in place. If your state does have legislation, check with www.BullyPolice.org to see how your legislation is rated. Some states rank very high and New Jersey has an A+++ rating. See how your bill compares and work with legislators to bring your state bill to the highest standards.

If your state does not have legislation on this subject, BullyPolice will help you strategize. In Kansas, we found that bringing young people to testify was very persuasive. Children telling their authentic stories are highly effective advocates.

Many bills have good language but lack accountability and funding components.

Collaborate with your state department of education to conduct an anonymous survey where school districts will be honest about the extent of planning, training, staffing, and programming they are actually sponsoring, in the face of an unfounded mandate.

Cyberbullying has been a controversial element of antibullying legislation in some states. It has been opposed in some areas because it holds the school responsible for situations away from school property. A spate of youth suicides in 2010 that were related to technology has been very persuasive in adding cyberbullying to the definition of bullying in legislation and school policies.

Gender orientation has also been a source of controversy. Sexual language has been tied to a number of school shootings and suicides, and cannot be ignored. Some bills define the particular issues for targets that need to be protected. Other bills focus on the bullying without specifying types of children that are at greater risk. The model New Jersey antibullying legislation, signed by a conservative governor has left no excuse to eliminate sexual words such as gay and lesbian to ensure that *all* schools must be safe for *all* children.

National Change Agents

Arne Duncan, appointed as Secretary of Education by President Barack Obama in 2009, has a vision for a radical change in our education system. Included in his numerous ideas are strategies to prevent bullying. A most significant concept is to give students ownership of the problem—with all the support possible from adults.

Kathleen Sebelius, Secretary of Health and Human Services, is his partner in this national bullying-prevention priority. The Department of Education and the Department of HHS co-sponsored the White House Conference on Bullying Prevention, which Fried attended. The Health Resources and Service Administration (HRSA) of HHS created a comprehensive campaign—"STOP BULLYING NOW! Take a Stand, Lend a Hand." The website www .stopbullyingnow.hrsa.gov. provides an exciting array of information, strategies, Tool Kits, and media campaigns, and is constantly updated.

Imagine a school where the administration has a clear vision of how to create a culture of compassion, caring, and citizenship that is a profound foundation for academic and personal success. Envision a school where teachers spend their time challenging eager minds, inspiring creativity, preparing young people for productive futures—freed from time-consuming discipline enforcement. Picture a school where students treat each other with respect; encourage each other to learn; and experience kindness, empathy, and interactions that do not lead to pain, rage, and revenge.

What if administrators, teachers, counselors, nonteaching staff, parents, and students shared the same vision and created a "Tipping Point" in their school? It can happen when Change Agents bring their passion to the dream and everyone becomes a champion for students in pain.

The Kindness Song

Words: SuEllen Fried
Music: SuEllen Fried,
Gary Adams

11

Empowering Students in the Solution

"I thought this was going to be one more boring lecture about bullying and I didn't want to be here. I can't believe what happened!"

—Steven, a student

The core component of the BullySafeUSA program that I, SuEllen Fried, founded in 2001 is the Student Empowerment Session (SES). The session consists of a series of questions, in a particular order, for students K–12, which has been tested over many years. There are variations for using the material, depending on the age level of the children.

I have trained over six hundred counselors, as well as health educators, teachers, child advocates, administrators, and parents to conduct this SES. The training process requires three days, and begins with an observation of me conducting the SES. It concludes on the third day with the participants facilitating their own SES with a group of students they do not know and observing a fellow participant facilitate a comparable session. Participants become committed to this concept of engaging children in a powerful dialogue because of its unique, effective approach to capture their interest and their collective wisdom.

To become a Certified BullySafeUSATrainer, it is necessary to participate in one of the three-day BullySafeUSA Training Institutes and then facilitate the SES with students for at least two consecutive years. Following that time period, the potential trainer must be observed by me or a Certified Trainer for final accreditation.

The SES has been evaluated by Andrew Terranova, PhD, Assistant Professor in the Department of Psychology at Stephen F. Austin State University in Texas. The evaluation is at the conclusion of this chapter.

I prefer to train school counselors for certification because they work with a variety of grade levels and develop their expertise with students of different age levels. As counselors, they are constantly on the lookout for research, films, videos, books, and other programs to round out their repertoire as they work with bullying and other student behavior issues. One of my Certified Trainers is a Second Step Trainer and another is a Certified Olweus Trainer. The BullySafeUSA program can be used in conjunction with other programs and/or approaches.

Prior to the publication of this book, the SES has never been made available without going through the training program. Understandably, a major concern is maintaining the quality of the delivery. Consequently, there are certain caveats that must be followed for the program to be effective.

The Socratic method of using questions as the process is absolutely essential.

It requires a role reversal where you, the facilitator, become the student and the students are expected to be your teachers. This is not a gambit. Students have a fund of information to divulge and you will become all the wiser when you take the time to listen to them. If you are not comfortable relinquishing your authority to conduct this session, it would not be wise to attempt this SES. The Institutes I have conducted usually have waiting lists of people who want to attend. On the one occasion, however, when administrators, teachers, and/or athletic coaches were assigned by their principal to go through this training, many acknowledged that this SES did not suit their style of student interaction.

All questions should be open-ended and allow for a multitude of answers.

This material is not presented as a test with students being rewarded for the correct answer. Every response is to be treated with respect. It is important to find a way to honor every reply. For instance, if a student gives a definition of emotional abuse when you ask for an example of verbal abuse, respond by saying: "That is going to come up when we talk about emotional abuse so be sure to raise your hand again."

Never allow students to ridicule any response by a fellow student.

The integrity of the program depends on making the session a safe, bully-free experience. If any bullying should occur, it should be used as a teachable moment. Humor can be a valuable tool to ease situations. Once verbal bullying has been defined, you can remind the students that put-downs, name-calling, snickering, and so on are forms of bullying and are not permitted.

STUDENT EMPOWERMENT SESSION ADVANCE PREPARATION

- It is best to work each session with children at the same grade level, that is, all of the fourth grade classes in a school together.
- The ideal number of students to work with is between forty and sixty. This program has been used successfully with as few as twenty and as many as 250. The larger the number of students, the more difficult it

is to make personal, eye-to-eye contact with every student and to bring the session to the conclusion that we seek.

- An intimate space—such as a classroom, the library, a music room, or even the stage of the auditorium is preferable to the cafeteria, the auditorium, or the gymnasium. The latter three present many challenges.
- Request one hour for the session at the elementary level—third through sixth. Forty to forty-five minutes is adequate for K–2 grades. Middle schools have a daily schedule that must be respected, usually forty-three to forty-seven minutes.
  The same is true of high schools. Occasionally, a middle-school principal will make the SES a high priority and arrange for an extended period of time. For grades K–2, I show a video, *Stop Teasing Me!* which can be ordered from Sunburst.
- Every student needs to wear a nametag with his or her first name only, printed in big, black letters. This must be specified or you may see pink and orange scrawled names that are unreadable.
- If you must work in a gymnasium, cafeteria, or auditorium, ask for a hand microphone that will allow you to move around the area.
- A school psychologist or counselor should be present for the sessions. Students might reveal personal data that should be followed up by school personnel.
- If a student discloses personal data that involves child abuse, a report must be made to someone in authority before leaving the school.
- The teachers of every class should be present during the SES, but out of view. When the session takes place in the classroom, teachers should not use the computer or grade papers during the session. Encourage them to listen carefully to their students' input.
- You will need paper or a blackboard and writing materials. There are a number of words and figures that you will want to be visible, such as the five kinds of bullying.
- It will not be possible to go through this entire sequence, allowing major time for student responses, in one hour, much less in forty-three minutes. I adapt each session to the needs of the particular group and determine spontaneously what needs to be eliminated, but this material includes the complete series of questions and demonstrations that I have used.
- Keep in mind that all children have developed in their particular environment and circumstances. If we could catch a glimpse of that context, we might have great admiration for their ability to endure, for their resourcefulness to meet their needs, and for their perseverance in the face of extraordinary obstacles.

STUDENT EMPOWERMENT SESSION

"Good morning, everyone. My name is SuEllen Fried." (Write your name on the blackboard or newsprint). "I am delighted to be with you and to have the opportunity to gather a lot of information from you. Most of the time we spend together, I will be asking you questions and I need you to be as honest and open as possible. Everything that is share will be kept confidential. To make sure that we have lots of participation without things getting out of hand, tell me what signal I should use to quiet things down. Thank You.

"When I ask a question and you raise your hand to give an answer, please correct me if I mispronounce your name. Names are very special and I want to honor yours.

"Here's my first question—how many of you have ever heard of child abuse?" (Most hands will go up.) "Who can tell me what child abuse is?" (Accept a few answers.) "You might be interested to know that when I was your age, the term child abuse didn't exist.

"For centuries, our society believed that children were the property of their parents who could do anything they wanted to with their offspring.

"In the 1970s we finally began passing laws to protect children but every child abuse law in this country specifies that abuse only occurs when the abuser is an adult. I believe that if a child is hurting, it doesn't matter if the person who is causing the pain is their parent or their classmate. If a child is suffering, it doesn't matter if the perpetrator is thirty-five or ten. I believe that bullying is a form of child abuse and no child deserves to be abused by anyone.

"Before I ask you any more questions, I want to apologize in advance because I am not going to be able to call on everyone who raises their hand for every question but I will do my best to call on everyone at some time during the session.

"The reason I am so concerned about bullying is because many years ago, I met a little girl named Kimberly Weisel. Kim was diagnosed with cancer when she was seven. How many of you know someone who has had cancer?" (Many hands will go up.) "Who can tell me what happens if you get cancer and you have chemotherapy?" (Someone will know that chemo causes your hair to fall out.) "That's a very important part of this story.

"Kim had chemo when she was seven and recovered but when she was ten, the cancer came back full force and the doctors decided that the best chance to save Kim's life was to have her spend her entire summer vacation in the hospital getting massive doses of chemo. I met Kim through my daughter, Paula, who worked at the hospital. Kim and Paula became very good friends and at the end of the summer, they both knew that Kim was not going to survive. Paula suggested that we invite Kim and her mom to come to our house for lunch to celebrate their friendship before they went back to their respective schools.

"While we were visiting and chatting, Paula asked Kim if she was looking forward to returning to school. Kim said, 'I can't wait for school to start! I haven't seen any of my friends all summer.' Then Paula asked Kim if she had any concerns about going back to school. Kim thought for a moment and said, 'Recess.' 'Why recess?' I asked. Kim explained that at recess there were some children who thought it was fun to pull her wig off of her head. When that happened, other children formed a circle around her and started pointing and laughing at her.

"I have never recovered from that conversation. I have never been able to put out of my mind a ten-year-old girl who was trying to figure out a way to let go of her life, her family, and her friends—and her biggest problem was peers at recess who thought it was amusing to make fun of her because she was bald because of cancer treatments.

"If students at Kim's school could be that cruel, I began to wonder if there were other schools where bullying was happening. I started going to schools and asking students, 'What are you doing to each other, why are you doing it, and what could we do to make it different?'

"One of the things I have learned is that there are five kinds of bullying—physical, verbal, emotional, sexual, and cyberbullying." (I do not include sexual bullying until the fourth grade. If third-grade students bring the subject up, accept their response. Some facilitators prefer to use the term *gender* bullying instead of *sexual* bullying.)

"What is physical bullying?" (Students will offer examples—kicking, hitting, punching, any body contact, etc. See chapter 4.)

"What is verbal bullying? Before you give examples, please complete the following sentence: 'sticks and stones can break your bones but . . .'" (Students will reply with "names can never hurt you.")

"Do you think that is true?" (Students will say 'No.')

"I would like to teach you a new sentence. 'Sticks and stones can break your bones but words can break your heart.' Please say that with me." (Students repeat.) "Who has had a broken bone?" (Hands go up.) "How long did it take your broken bone to heal?" (This is a good opportunity to call on someone who hasn't participated, but you won't have time to call on everyone.)

"Broken bones can take a few weeks, a few months, sometimes a year to heal. How long does it take to heal a broken heart?" (Students will reply 'Never' or 'Forever.')

"Now tell me, what is verbal bullying?" (Students will give examples—name-calling, put-downs, etc. See chapter 4. If 'gossip,' 'spreading rumors,' 'betraying a secret' are not mentioned, be sure to state those examples.)

"What is emotional bullying? Give me examples of bullying where there is no physical contact and no words are spoken." (Students will offer examples—rolling your eyes, sending notes, using the third finger, body language, etc. See chapter 4. If 'excluding someone' is not mentioned, be sure to talk about leaving someone out, not letting someone sit next to you on the bus, rejecting, and isolating. If you have time, tell the story of the birthday party when no one came.)

"What is sexual bullying?" (Students will give examples of touching someone where they shouldn't be touched, making fun of someone's body, etc. See chapter 4. This is uncomfortable for many students so acknowledge that this is a squirmy subject but very important to discuss. If students are still reluctant, mention examples that you have learned from other students. Sexual language MUST be discussed.)

"There is a form of sexual bullying that we need to discuss—sexual language—using words like 'gay,' 'queer,' 'homo'—you know what I'm talking about, don't you?" (Heads will nod.)

"The reason I am willing to stand here and say these words is that many of the school shootings happened because of those words. Boys in prison who committed murders have told interviewers that being called those words, over and over, pushed them over the edge. I plead with you to give up this lethal language. I do not want to read about one more student who has been killed by a classmate because of sexual words.

"What is cyberbullying?" (Students will give examples, saying mean things about someone in a chat room, stealing someone's password, putting stuff on Facebook, Formspring, Myspace, sexting, etc.) "It is so cowardly and cruel to torment someone anonymously and then send the messages to untold numbers. Targets have no way to defend themselves against such widespread abusive communication. You need to know that technology has become very sophisticated to track down the senders of such messages and cyber bulliers will not be exempt from discovery.

"Now, I want you to vote on which form of bullying you feel is most common at your school. Physical?" (Take vote.) "Verbal?" (Take vote.) "Emotional?" (Take vote.) "Sexual?" (Take vote.) "Cyberbullying?" (Take vote.)

(Physical bullying gets few or no votes. Fights are obvious and intervention occurs almost immediately. That is not the case with verbal bullying, which invariably receives the most votes. Emotional bullying receives a sprinkling amount of votes from students, but receives the most votes from teachers and adults who are present during the session. Sexual bullying and cyberbullying also receive a smattering of votes, but something changes dramatically when the next question is posed.)

"Which kind of bullying do you think causes the most stress or concern for targets?"

(There has been a consistent vote all across the country by students for sexual bullying. Middle-school students have always identified sexual bullying as a major issue, but in the last several years, even fourth, fifth, and sixth graders are casting their votes for sexual bullying. More recently, however, votes for cyberbullying, especially among middle-school students, have increased.)

"Bullying causes pain and I want to share something I've learned. I'm going to draw this on the board for you." (Draw PAIN, RAGE, REVENGE cycle from chapter 1.)

"Pain doesn't evaporate, it doesn't disappear. It collects, and when enough pain collects, it turns to Rage. And then the Rage can become Revenge. Revenge causes Pain and the cycle starts all over again! This cycle doesn't just happen in schools; it happens between religions, and tribes and countries and becomes a global problem. We must stop pain, wherever and whenever we see it if we want to make the world a peaceful planet."

(Draw the PAIN, DEPRESSION, SUICIDE cycle from chapter 1 on the board.) "A boy came up to me after a session like this and he told me that I needed to draw another cycle—Pain, Depression, and Suicide. He told me that when he is in pain, he doesn't become aggressive, he becomes Depressed, and when he gets Depressed he starts thinking about Suicide. He told me that the only reason he hasn't committed suicide is because of the pain it would cause his parents."

(Draw third cycle on the board—the one that is the combination of the first two from chapter 1.) "Months later, a young boy observed my two drawings, and told me that I needed to figure out a different drawing—one that combined the two. He told me that some days he wakes up and wants to get even with everyone who has tormented him and the next day he just wants to stay in bed, pull the covers over his head and think about doing away with himself. Please do everything you can to stop pain.

"We need to talk about targets, bulliers, and witnesses. I am very concerned about targets." (Write the word "targets" on the blackboard.) "One hundred and sixty thousand children stay home from school every day because they are afraid of what might happen to them on the bus, the playground, the cafeteria, the bathrooms. There are more and more students who are showing up in doctor's offices with headaches and stomachaches and depression because of the way they are being treated by their classmates. There are students who are committing suicide because of bullying. There is even a new word that describes this action and it will probably end up in the next edition of the dictionary. The word is 'bullycide.'

"I am also concerned about bulliers." (Write the word "bulliers"on the blackboard.) "Over thirty years ago, a very wise researcher by the name of Dr. Leonard Eron was concerned about bullying. He persuaded a school district that had 875 students in the third grade to allow him to conduct a survey. They printed out the names of every third-grade student and then asked every student to take a pencil and put a check mark in front of the name of every student they thought was a bullier. All the students made their check marks, and the papers were collected and put away in a filing cabinet for ten years.

"When the third graders became seniors, the process was repeated. All the names of the seniors were printed out and the students were asked to make a check mark in front of the name of any student they considered to be a bullier. When the researchers compared the two lists, they learned that almost all seniors who received a check mark had received a check mark when they were in the third grade. Nothing had changed in ten years.

"The researchers were curious to see what was going to happen to those bulliers when they became adults so they waited ten more years and found a significant number of the people who had been identified as bulliers when they were in school. What they discovered was that *one* out of every *four* bulliers checked on the survey had a criminal record by the time they reached thirty years of age. The males were more likely to become men who abused their wives and the females were at greater risk to become mothers who abused their own children. Bulliers not only hurt other people, they hurt themselves even more.

"Witnesses are the key to the solution of bullying." (Write the word "witnesses" on the board and circle it.) "How many of you have seen some of the law shows on TV? Then you know that a witness is someone who sees what happens and has to tell the truth. Here's another study. Researchers went into a school and asked the teachers how frequently they intervened in bullying situations. Seventy-one percent of teachers say they almost always intervene in bullying situations. When the students were asked about teacher intervention, they reported that teachers intervene only 25 percent of the time. We think the difference in the perception is not that teachers don't *care*, it's that they aren't *there*. But witnesses, you are there!

"Because you are there, we need you to get involved. I need seven volunteers to help me with an exercise about witnesses." (Hand each of the seven students a card and ask them to form a line in front of the class. Each card contains a different statement: Tell an Adult. Don't Give Bulliers Power. Include a Target in Your Activities. Challenge the Bullier. Befriend a Troubled Bullier. Support a Target in Private. Get a Group to Challenge the Bullier.)

"These are actions you could take as a witness. Please read all of them and tell me which one is the most risky." ("Challenge the Bullier" is invariably mentioned as the riskiest.) "Will the person with "Challenge the Bullier" please move to the front of the line? What is the next riskiest?" (Continue asking students to tell which is the next riskiest until all seven students have moved to places in the order of most to least risky. The middle five will vary each time but "Support a Target in Private" usually ends up as the least risky. Affirm all responses.) "Thank you very much. Challenging the bully can be very risky. I'm not asking you to do anything that makes you uncomfortable, but there is one thing that every one of you can do and it's very important. Talk to a target when no one else is around." (Ask for a student to volunteer to be a target. Turn to that student and say the following words: "You don't deserve to be treated this way. I'm so sorry I can't make it stop." Ask the student to share with the class how it felt to hear those words. The student will confirm how much it means to hear that someone else is aware of what is happening and believes that it is wrong.)

"Some students have told me that they wanted to report what was happening to an adult, but they were afraid they would be accused of being a snitch or a tattletale." (Write "tattling" and "reporting" on the board. Ask students to tell what the difference is. Accept all answers and if it hasn't been given report the following: 'Many students have said that tattling is when you are trying to get someone IN trouble' [draw an arrow going down] 'and reporting is when you are trying to get someone OUT of trouble' [Draw an arrow going up.])

"Here's an important question. Why does someone become a bullier?" (Students will say: "Bullies have problems in their family, they're being abused at home, an older brother or sister is picking on them, they want revenge, they need attention, they want to be popular, they're bored, they're mean and nobody makes them stop, they've seen something on TV or on video games and they're copying it, they don't know how to handle their anger, they can get away with it, they're scared inside and they don't want others to know it so they act tough, maybe someone in their family has died or is very sick or their parents are getting a divorce and they can't handle the pain, they don't feel good about themselves so they want others to suffer, they think it's cool, they're jealous, they have a 'crush' on someone and pick on them to get their attention, they don't have self esteem, they want power, their parents never taught them what was right and what was wrong, they're involved with drugs or alcohol, they want to control everybody else because they can't control themselves.")

"Your comments are extremely insightful. You are saying that bulliers are very troubled, that they are needy and have lots of problems.

"This is a good time to share a story with you about a group of fish. This story comes from a book by Dr. Karl Menninger, *The Human Mind* (1971). Dr. Karl told about a group of fish who were swimming in a pond. They came upon a fish who was upside down and it was flapping its tail. The group of fish thought that was really weird so they swam away from the flapping fish as quickly as they could.

"The reason the fish was upside down and flapping its tail was because it had a hook in its mouth and it was doing the best thing it could do. Dr. Karl went on to say that there are a lot of people who have hooks in their mouths that are invisible to us and if we could see their hook, we might appreciate that they are doing the best they can, considering the circumstances that they are in.

"I want to talk with you about why someone becomes a target. Usually students will say because they are *different* so over the years I have collected a list of *differentnesses.*

"Because you're too tall, too short, too heavy, too thin, too rich, too poor, too smart, too slow, different color hair or skin, or religion or culture, just moved from another school, wear glasses, have braces, clothes are not fashionable, parents are divorced, like poetry instead of football—the list goes on and on and on. What I have learned from this list is that everyone fits into at least one of these categories. Therefore we are all different. So, if everyone is different, there has to be another reason why targets get picked on. I think it's because some students are getting pleasure out of being mean. If you want to cause pain for someone, you will always be able to find something about them to ridicule. The issue is not who is different, but why does someone think it's cool to be cruel.

"If you are getting pleasure out of causing pain, you have some work you need to do and we need to help you.

"I would like to know what you have learned about how to stop bullying. What can you do?" (Write answers on board. One of the first responses will be "ignore.") "How many of you have ever ignored a bullier and it worked? How many of you have ever ignored a bullier and it didn't work? What works on one bullier may not work on the next so you have to have a lot of options." (Write down all answers as quickly as possible. If someone says "fight back" you have to stop and deal with that response.) "I have heard from some students that fighting back was the only strategy that worked but I have to share my concern with you. This is a true story that was told to me by the Deputy Attorney General of Delaware, Rhonda Denny.

"There was a target who had been abused relentlessly by a bullier. The bullying was physical and verbal and it got progressively worse. The target stuffed his anger for months and months and finally one day he couldn't take it any more and he punched the bullier in the face. The bullier fell back against a concrete pillar and was knocked unconscious. He was rushed to the hospital and fell into a coma. For a while they were not sure that he was going to live. He did survive, but if he hadn't, the target who punched him could have been charged with manslaughter and ended up in a prison setting for years. The risks of fighting are too serious and I am hoping that you will find another way to handle the pain.

"I want to talk to you about the difference between the way girls and boys bully. I have heard that there are five major differences and I would like some feedback from you. When I mention each difference, please nod your heads up and down if you agree, and sideways if you disagree.

"The first difference I've heard is that boys are more physical and sexual and girls are more verbal and emotional and probably more into cyberbullying." (Look for head nods. If there is a lot of disagreement, ask for comments.)

"The second difference I've heard is that boys are more direct and in your face and girls are more indirect and behind your back." (Look for head nods.)

"The third difference I've heard is that if a couple of boys get into a conflict, five minutes later they will go skateboarding together. When girls get into a conflict, it goes on and on and on." (Look for head nods.)

"The fourth difference I've heard is that when boys pick on each other, it's usually one on one but when girls bully, they get a clique or a whole group to hurt someone." (Look for head nods.)

"The fifth difference I've heard is that when boys bully, they pick on someone outside of their circle of friends. When girls bully, they turn on their closest friends." (Look for head nods.)

"Ladies, young women, why are we so hard on each other? This meanness has to stop. Life is tough enough, as it is. We are not on this Earth to tear each other down. That is not the purpose of our lives. Please stop the pain!

"I'm going to teach you a word. Some of you may know it, but it has been my experience that very few students can give a good definition of the word 'empathy.'

"Empathy is the capacity to put yourself in somebody else's situation and imagine how it would be to walk in their shoes. If you broke your leg and had to walk on crutches and you see someone walking with crutches, you know what they're going through. But if your friend's parents are getting a divorce and your parents are not getting a divorce, you can still imagine how painful, how stressful that is for your friend. That is empathy!

"Empathy is so important that I am going to ask you to practice it, right now. Please close your eyes. I want you to think about someone you know who is a target and I want you to put yourself in his or her place. Concentrate on what it would feel like to be that person." (Allow twelve to fifteen seconds to pass.)

"I'm impressed with the way you focused. Now, I am going to ask the last question and the first person that raises his or her hand to answer this question must have a lot of courage, so wait until you hear the question before you raise your hand. Because of everything we have talked about together this morning and all the feelings that are going through your minds, is there someone in this room that would like to do some healing? Is there someone in this room who would be willing to apologize and make amends for something that you have done or said?"

(Most often several hands will go up. If no hands go up, wait a few seconds and allow silence to work its pressure. If no hands go up at that point, try another approach.) "What usually happens at this point is that one person will serve as a role model and as soon as they share an apology, a lot of hands will go up and we won't have time to hear them."

(When John or Mary raises their hand, go stand by that student.)

"Who is the person you wish to apologize to?" (Student will say: "I want to apologize to Ben." Ask where Ben is and go to him.) "Ben, John has apologized to you. Do you accept his apology?" (Student will accept the apology.) "Thank you, John and thank you, Ben. You have given us a valuable lesson in remorse and forgiveness. Thank you very, very much. There is a world of difference between 'I apologize' and 'I'm sorry.' Many people say 'I'm sorry' and then they do the same thing and then they say 'I'm sorry' and they do it again. An apology is a commitment to change your behavior. John is not going to cause pain for Ben anymore." (Call on any others who have raised their hands and repeat the process of honoring and thanking. If someone will not accept the apology, ask the person who apologized if they can understand why the apology has not been accepted. Then return to the person who received the apology and ask how long it would take for them to believe that a new behavior is genuine. Take that figure back to the person who apologized and negotiate a time frame for trust to be established.)

"I'm so sorry that we have run out of time for individual apologies. The rest of you will have to apologize in private but it will still be very meaningful. Would everyone in this room who made an apology, please stand up? It took a lot of courage to admit you had been hurtful and to make amends. Thank you very much.

"Would everyone in this room who owes someone an apology, please stand up?" (Many will stand.) "Please make sure that you apologize to the person who deserves it. Would everyone in this room who feels that they deserve an apology, please stand up?" (Some will stand.) "Look around the room and if you are someone who has caused pain for people who are standing, make amends. It will make you feel a lot better, and it will help someone else to heal. When you stop the pain, you are doing your part to change the world.

"Now I have a request for everyone in this class. If you notice that some students in this class are being kinder, that they are changing their behavior, please compliment them in your own creative way. It is not easy to change habits, so if someone is making an effort, honor their good work by letting them know you are a witness.

"I would like to tell you one more story. I read about a boy in California who developed cancer, had chemotherapy, and all of his hair fell out. He decided to drop out of school because he didn't want to be picked on. When his classmates heard about this, thirteen boys went to the barbershop and had their heads shaved so this young man could come to school without dread. Whenever I think about those thirteen boys, it makes me very proud to be a human being. That is the capacity that we have to care about each other.

"Thank you so much for all that you have taught me. I'm deeply grateful."

End of Session

I want to share one example of the thousands of apologies I have witnessed. At a middle school, a sixth-grade boy, Howard, raised his hand and apologized to the entire class. He said: "I know I get really angry sometimes and I say terrible things. I have ADHD and it's not my fault that I'm different. I get very upset when you make fun of me. Everything is so much harder for me because of my problems. No one in this room would want to change places with me. I wish you would just leave me alone."

He reduced everyone to tears with his honesty and courage—students, teachers, counselors, administrators, and me. I checked back with the counselor and learned that students did stop, or at least greatly reduced bullying toward Howard. He was extremely happy. He now attends an alternative school where his disabilities can be better met.

TIPS ON THE STUDENT EMPOWERMENT SESSION

The biggest challenge you will have is time! You won't be able to get everything in, especially if you have an enthusiastic class and lots of students who wish to participate. You need to allow ten minutes, at the least, to do the empathy/apology section. Every single minute is precious. Explain to the person in charge that you need for the session to start on time. It takes practice to own this content and make decisions on the spot with each unique group of students. You will get better with each session.

My best and worst experiences have happened in middle schools. I can usually tell from the responses to the first question whether the class is going to be a challenge. In some situations, I decide not to present the empathy/close your eyes/apology piece.

Instead, I will read two or three "Letters from Children" that are in chapter 14 of my book *Bullies, Targets, & Witnesses*. There are six such letters that have a Stickiness Factor.

When participants observe me conducting a session on the first morning of the Training Institute, they can't believe they will be able to make this work when they are facilitators on the third morning. They discover that not only does it work for them, but their partners have a successful experience as well. Cherish the privilege of being in the presence of young people who deserve a "cleansing experience."

What is most important about a SES is to engage the students in a dialogue. They have received lectures and speeches. Your gift is to empower them to contribute the information.

A&E produced a Bill Kurtis Investigative Report entitled "Bullied to Death" in 2000. I was featured in that report and you can see a small segment of my work with students, which can be ordered from Amazon.com.

A full-length, one-hour training DVD of me conducting a SES can be ordered through my website, www.bullysafeusa.com.

I would love to hear from you. Please send me e-mails and notes about your sessions. suellenfried@hotmail.com. SuEllen Fried, P.O. Box 8527, Prairie Village, KS, 66208.

EVALUATION HIGHLIGHTS

BullySafeUSA is a comprehensive school-based bullying intervention program designed to reduce bullying and promote prosocial behavior.

The BullySafeUSA program includes a Student Empowerment Session and follow-up activities with students grades K–12. Students will learn the five kinds of bullying—physical, verbal, emotional, sexual, and cyberbullying. They will learn about the roles of the target, the bullier, and the witness and how those roles interchange. An emphasis on actions that witnesses can take is a key component. A new saying: "Sticks and stones can break your bones, but words can break your heart" is introduced. Students will learn strategies for dealing with bulliers, the difference between tattling and reporting, differences between the ways girls and boys bully, and will be taught a strong segment on empathy.

They will understand bullying is a form of child abuse: peer-to-peer abuse. A goal of the program is to change the culture of the school by reducing the pain, rage, revenge cycle that is connected to bullying. Staff training and parent seminars are offered to support the student empowerment session. An activities guide, "30 Activities for Getting Better at Getting Along" will reinforce the anticipated attitude and behavior changes.

To evaluate the effectiveness of the BullySafeUSA program, a program evaluation was conducted in the southeastern United States. Data were collected from approximately two hundred students participating in the BullySafeUSA program and approximately two hundred students from nearby schools who were not participating in any systematic bullying intervention. Students in both the treatment and comparison groups completed surveys at the beginning and end of the school year. Shortly after the initial assessment, students in the treatment group began participating in the BullySafeUSA program.

BULLYSAFEUSA

Executive Summary of Positive Program Evaluation Findings

- Students participating in the BullySafeUSA program learned the material presented in the program. They doubled their factual knowledge about bullying after participating in the program for a few months, and after continued participation, on average they were able to correctly respond to 80 percent of questions about bullying.

- Students participating in the BullySafeUSA program felt an increased sense of responsibility to help the targets of bullying. While approximately half of students indicated that a witness should always help a target before the intervention, over 75 percent of students indicated that they should always help the targets of bullying after participating in the BullySafeUSA Program. Students who were not participating in any bullying prevention program evidenced no change in their sense of responsibility to help the targets.
- Over the course of the school year, students participating in the BullySafeUSA program continued to feel that there were things they could do to resolve the conflict when the targets of bullies. Students who did not participate in the program felt less control as the school year progressed.
- Over the course of the school year, students participating in the BullySafeUSA program continued to report incidents of bullying to teachers. Students who were participating in the BullySafeUSA program reported incidents of bullying less and less as the school year progressed. By the end of the school year, on average they were almost never reporting bullying.
- Relative to students who were not participating in a prevention program, the students participating in the BullySafeUSA intervention evidenced significant reduction in peer victimization. Peer victimization experiences decreased by 23 percent in students participating in the BullySafeUSA program. Reductions were apparent in both social and physical victimization.
- Whereas students participating in the BullySafeUSA program evidenced a 15 percent reduction in bullying behaviors, students not participating in any bullying prevention program evidenced 26 percent increase in these bullying behaviors over the same time period.

Evaluation Coordinated by
Andrew Terranova, PhD
Assistant Professor, Department of Psychology
Stephen F. Austin State University
Box 13046 – SFA Station
Nacogdoches, TX 75962
E-Mail: terranova@sfasu.edu
Telephone: (936) 468–1483

12

Ten Burning Questions Posed by Educators

Recently, Fried gave several bullying workshops at a conference for the California Association of Private Schools Organization (CAPSO). She asked the participants to jot down on a slip of paper one "burning question" they would like her to address. To her complete amazement, with the exception of one request, every single attendee wanted to know how to deal with parents who won't believe their child is a bullier. Consequently, this will be our first question. The other questions have surfaced frequently and are quoted directly as we polled educators across the country.

#1 "How do you handle the parents of a child who won't accept that their child is a bully?"

As may be expected, many parents of children who engage in all forms of bullying behavior are bulliers themselves. They serve as role models for their children's actions and may even encourage their children to be aggressive. The children may hear: "Don't you ever let anyone take advantage of you or put you down." These parents may be the third or fourth generation of people who grew up in an aggressive environment or they may have had painful experiences as targets when they were young and are determined to spare their children that pain. Regardless of the history, we make the following recommendations.

The first is a one-on-one session with the parent(s). Do not use the term "bully" or "bullying" in your communication! Begin the conversation by discussing the positive behaviors or skills that you have observed in their child. Then announce that you and the parent want this year to be the most successful possible for their child. You will be partners to make that happen and it is essential to share important information with each other. The parent will know some things about the student that you don't know, and you might know some things about their child that they don't know since you see their child in a different setting. Ask the parent to give you information that would be helpful for you to know. Listen attentively and affirm their report. Then bring up some specific behaviors that have come to your attention. Be *very* specific without using the term "bullying."

Emphasize that it is your responsibility to keep every student in your class safe. Report how you have handled the situations and express your concern if the behavior is continuing. Talk about the school Code of Conduct and how you are expected to deal with infractions. Ask the parent for their input before you proceed to the next level of consequence. Remind the parent that you are partners and you both want a positive resolution. Come up with a mutually agreed upon action plan that both you and the parent support and suggest that you talk again in a few weeks to keep current on any progress.

Do all that you can to keep the parent as an ally to make this a successful year. If the parent becomes belligerent, suggest that you both think about the conversation, what you have heard from each other and agree to have another meeting at a future date. On that occasion, ask the school counselor or an administrator to be present to support your perspective and concern for other children. Explain the steps that will be taken to avoid suspension or expulsion. You might recommend an appointment with a physician or a therapist for some testing. Maintain how important it is to deal with issues before they become more severe.

You might gain some support from a parent by asking if similar behaviors of concern would be acceptable in the workplace. If childhood is a training ground for adulthood, it becomes easier to see what is acceptable and what isn't.

The second option that we recommend is a meeting with all of the parents. Be as insistent as possible that at least one caregiver attend. Many parents of bulliers have been characterized as abusive themselves. These parents might bring the same personality traits to the classroom when meeting with teachers. In truth, however, parents of the targets will be more inclined to attend such a session.

The agenda for the meeting should include a discussion of the importance of having a bully-free classroom. Share some background on the concept of peer abuse and the five different types. Talk about how important it is for parents and teachers to work together and relay research confirming that children are more successful when such cooperation is taking place. Also discuss the fact that many parents don't realize their child is a bullier or a target and therefore it is essential to know what to look for and how to help their child. Be sure to apprise parents of the steps that will be taken if bullying is reported—either by parents or students. For a suggested meeting outline, see our website.

If the parents of the bulliers do not attend the class meeting, then you have good reason to contact them for a private meeting to report to them what was discussed at the class meeting. Follow the suggestions for the one-on-one meeting.

#2 "What should I do about a colleague who is a bully?"

Developing a professional code of ethics with the faculty is an effective way of establishing that the school will hold educators accountable for their behavior. Observations have been made that teachers who bully are often new teachers reacting to overwhelming frustrations or tenured teachers who are very set in their ways. It is the responsibility of the principal to deal with a teacher who bullies students. There are principals who know of staff members who engage in bullying but because of tenure cannot dismiss them. Many principals have shared their frustrations and their efforts to move these teachers into office positions where they will not be with students in the classroom. Principals who do not have the power to terminate inappropriate teachers are eager to find a solution. We have several suggestions to offer:

For the new teacher, assign an experienced teacher to be a Collegial Coach. This new teacher can confide in the coach for mentoring without fear of reprisal. Teachers who have learned the ropes of classroom management can share effective techniques for maintaining order and preventing stressful issues from arising. The following website offers extensive resources on the topic: www.northern.edu/ois/Mentor.htm.

For issues with the tenured teacher, schedule a staff training session on the subject of bullying prevention and insist that the trainer cover this specific topic. It is best to have an outside trainer who can make generic recommendations without knowing the particular teachers. The core of the training is to focus on changing the culture—by changing attitudes, feelings, and behaviors. While children are the focus of these changes, every adult must model these changes. We cannot have expectations for students that adults are not prepared to honor for themselves.

At this training, recommend that when any staff member, including nonteaching staff, *witnesses* a teacher bullying a student, they are to report that documented information to the principal. If we are asking student witnesses to take risks, staff members must be willing to do the same. The principal can use the collection of documented reports to contact the teacher.

An unexpected solution came when Mary Fischer, a BullySafeUSA colleague, was conducting a Student Empowerment Session. Toward the end, a teacher who had been listening intently to the definitions and descriptions of bullying spontaneously apologized to her students for her bullying behavior. The forgiving students, who were so touched by her repentance, rushed to give her hugs and a tearful conclusion was had by all. Mary reports that the atmosphere of the classroom completely changed, and the teacher, her students, and their parents enjoyed a splendid year. The power of an adult apologizing to a student or students is inestimable.

A final recommendation is that the following e-mail that Fried received from a student be copied and placed in every teacher's mailbox. It is reprinted without grammar, punctuation or spelling corrections.

I wanted some information regarding a teacher who is the bully in her classroom to students as young as I. I am depressed and get sweats right before I go into her classroom. My mother and the principal is aware of this teachers lacks but the teacher still abuses us in her class, the principle said that it is very hard to get rid of a teacher even if they know that this teacher is not fit to teach, this teacher has files of complaints from kids and parents but nothing is been looked on. Am I the only kid in the world that has a teacher who bullies? Are my classmates now, before me and after me will have no choice to just deal with the abusive ways, because it is just too much work or details to go through just to discipline a teacher, it is just not fair. This teacher has been teaching more than 25 years as my mom had her once and it was an unpleasant experience for her too and I am experiencing it. I just feel very strongly that this is so unfair, that teachers can do to us and say things that hurt our feelings and that is okay, if we the student did any of that disrespect to the teacher we encounter almost an world war III from the principle, teachers, and parents while this teacher do to us and just laughs. I don't want nothing to do with science anymore, I also don't respect teachers as much as I did, I always respected them like a second parent but this teacher changed almost all my thinking of my mind. Can you help me? Do you have any materials I can share with my classmates and may be help the principle to do something about our problem? This is a pro-bully for she have been doing it for almost 30 years. 20, 30 thousands had to endure her and more,

I pray for my teacher to STOP. She makes us cry every time.

#3 "How do I handle a group of girl bullies who are a real challenge?"

A spate of books, such as *Queen Bees and Wannabees: Helping Your Daughter Survive Cliques, Gossip, Boyfriends, and the New Realities of Girl World* (2009) and *Odd Girl Out: The Hidden Culture of Aggression in Girls* (2002) and movies such as *Mean Girls* have added a whole new dimension to our understanding of the term "relational aggression." RA, as it is widely used, is a type of psychological abuse in which harm is caused through or to relationships. Carol Gilligan (1982) argues that boys are socialized to value achievement as their most important goal while girls are socialized to value affiliation as their most important goal.

Because it is related to increased depression, lower academic performance, increased suicidal ideation, increased anger, and sadness, it must be confronted. Friendships, relationships, and affiliations dominate female behavior. Beginning in preschool, little girls use "I won't be your friend" as their strongest leverage to get what they want. As they grow older, the more covert they become, but the threat is the same.

We believe in confronting girls about their cruelty by discussing the five differences between the way girls and boys bully as described in chapter 11. Preferably, at the beginning of the year—or sadly, when a crisis occurs—a teacher, perhaps with a counselor, could invite all the girls in the class to have a lunch in the classroom. If this is an elementary class, try to create an intimate atmosphere. Ask the Physical Education teacher to keep the boys for at least a forty-five-minute to an hour period. Push the chairs out of the way, spread several blankets on the floor and create an informal atmosphere. For middle-school girls, you will need to orchestrate a more sophisticated session, but try to make it as informal as possible.

Start the session with some kind of an "ice-breaker" that rearranges their typical groupings. One example is to ask all of the girls who are the oldest in their family to sit together, the middle children to sit together, the youngest child to sit together and the only children to sit together. Direct them to share with each other what's good and not-so-good about their birth order.

After a few minutes bring all the girls together in a circle and begin a new conversation by asking girls to mention women in their lives that they admire. Pick up on the caring, nurturing, generous qualities that are mentioned and talk about what gifts loving women bring to the world.

Then bring up the "five differences" between the way girls and boys bully and ask if there is any truth to the statements. Ask if any of them have sisters or close friends who have known what that feels like. Gently lead them into a more personal conversation about hurtfulness they have witnessed or experienced. Ask them what they can do to stop the pain.

When girls can recognize how much they resort to sabotage and backstabbing to cause pain, how capricious they are in the way they banish a longstanding friendship, admit that a slight can grow into a schism and last for years without resolution, and acknowledge that a clique can supply the courage to do and say things you never would do on your own, they can begin to examine their behavior and make change.

The Ophelia Project and Girl Scouts USA have developed wonderful materials and programs. Bringing the mothers and daughters together to experience a reading group with each other can serve a multitude of purposes. Choose a book appropriate for the ages of the girls.

#4 "How can I help a student understand that she or he is bullying others?"

Perhaps the question should be reframed. The real question is "How can I help a student to choose more successful behavior?" If all behavior serves a purpose, what is the student gaining by being hurtful to others? The solution is not to coerce the student to admit that they are "bad" or that they are a "bully" but to discover their intention.

Arrange to spend some private time with the student and approach the conversation with the visualization of the student with a "hook in his or her mouth." Is the student acting out in an attempt to avoid pain of some kind? Is some reward being given for the behavior? Is the student under a lot of stress and taking it out on other people? Is the student acting out because of a lack of empathy or a moral code? The student is probably expecting you to make some judgment about him or her. Instead you are trying to understand what the student needs and how you can help him or her meet that need. Ask questions to get at the motivation.

If you can reach a point where the student believes you are coming from concern for him or her as well as for others, you can focus on the unaccept-able behaviors. Always refer to the specific behaviors and never use the term "bully" or "bullying." Ask if the student feels like he or she has ever crossed the line. Be sure to bring empathy into the discussion. Express belief that the student has the power to control inappropriate behavior. Sometimes students run out of impulse control at the end of the day. Create a special hand signal that you can use with each other for times of stress and times of praise. When the student is getting stressed and about to lose control, have him or her give you a hand signal. Ask the student to take a message to the office. Make a prior contact with the secretary so she understands that the student is com-ing to the office for stress relief. When you notice that the student is exerting self-control, give a special hand signal to let the student know you are aware.

#5 "How can I get students to report when they are being bullied or when they witness others being bullied?"

We have addressed this in different sections of our book but we will pull together several recommendations that we have made. First and foremost have a class meeting on the subject of bullying. A Student Empowerment Session has made a dramatic difference for thousands of students.

Issues of confidentiality must be discussed and the person reported to has to earn credibility with the students. Assure all of the students that a reporter of abusive behavior will not be put in jeopardy by divulging their report to the offender. Remind students of how many tragedies have been averted when reports have been made to adults.

Have a discussion about the difference between *tattling* and *reporting*. Remind the students that tattling is when you are trying to get someone IN trouble and reporting is when you are trying to get someone OUT of trouble. At the elementary-school level, it might take repeating the question many times before it becomes the new social norm. With older children, train them to work with younger children on this issue. By working on this topic with younger students, they will come to a better understanding of how important it is to reach out to adults. Also, stress the consequences for our society when criminals are protected by people who won't "snitch." Explain that logically, the more students who report, the less likely it will be for the offender to know who was the source. Share some stories about adults who still carry wounded consciences because of hurting students they never protected.

Assure targets that it is not a weakness to involve adults. Students who bully have problems and they make problems for targets that require adult intervention. It is far worse to suffer regularly, to lose confidence and self-esteem, to dread coming to school, and to become depressed or filled with rage. Schools are obligated to provide a safe environment for all students and that includes eliminating bullying.

You might also want to do the Witness Training exercise from chapter 11 if your class has not participated in a Student Empowerment Session.

At all costs, never dismiss a report that may have required a great deal of courage to be given to you. Honor it with trust and respect.

#6 "How do I respond when I observe students taunting classmates by calling them gay, queer, or other derogatory sexual terms?"

In a survey conducted by the National Education Association in 2010, data was collected from a nationally representative sample of both teachers and education support professionals (ESPs). Both groups indicated a greater need for additional training related to sexual orientation and gender issues.

It is imperative that all adults—teachers, ESPs, administrators, and parents—overcome their reluctance to directly deal with the sexual language that not only includes "gay" and "queer," but other words we have previously identified such as "faggot," "homo," "slut," "lesbo," "whore," "ho," and more. We used to be tentative about stating some of these words if they were not forthcoming from the students, but circumstances have changed our reluctance. In many cases of multiple school shootings, the particular form of taunting that pushed boys over the edge was the relentless tagging of some sexually pejorative term. This language has become too lethal—both as a cause of peer murders and peer suicides—to make allowances for our discomfort.

Dave Reynolds is the Senior Public Policy and Research Manager with The Trevor Project in California. The Trevor Project is the leading national organization focused on crisis and suicide prevention efforts among lesbian, gay, bisexual, transgender, and questioning youth. When I contacted him for a response to question #6, he replied: "Language that is derisive toward lesbian, gay, bisexual, transgender, and questioning young people creates an unhealthy learning environment for all students, not only those involved in the incident. The best thing to do is to address anti-LGBTQ language directly and consistently every time you hear it."

These are challenging issues to address and we know of teachers and administrators who would prefer to avoid them altogether. The fact that students consistently raise these issues with us, often taking great risks in front of their peers to do so, compels us to match their courage with our own. Too many children pay a price for our unwillingness to confront the sexual bullying that happens in our schools.

We suggest that teachers take a proactive position on sexual language. Initiate the discussion BEFORE it comes to your attention. Take a strong stand about the negative consequences and declare your commitment to eliminate words that have actually caused the deaths of students. If you do overhear them, intervene immediately.

#7 "What if my principal doesn't support me when I am trying to deal with bullying situations?"

Invite the principal to attend a Student Empowerment Session or to sit in on a brief class discussion that you lead about bullying. Be sure to cover the five types of bullying. Come up with some questions for the students that you think will produce the most persuasive argument for your concerns.

Most school counselors are very attuned to bullying problems. Enlist your counselor to work with you on a convincing strategy to grab your principal's interest. Will it be parent anger, or the threat of a lawsuit, or the competitive challenge of another school in the district that is making great strides in bullying prevention? Research the particular angle that will have the most impact on your principal's decision.

Give your students a writing assignment about bullying. Have them give examples of bullying they have experienced or witnessed. Have them include bullying incidents on the bus, the playground, the cafeteria, the bathroom, and other hot spots. Ask them to give some suggestions on how the school should handle bullying problems. Be sure to protect their privacy. Share the essays with the principal.

Explain to the principal how you intend to design a bullying-prevention plan for your classroom, based on the information you have collected from your students and their parents. List some very specific support you believe would be helpful to your vision, maybe just one item to begin with. Keep the principal informed of the progress you are making with your plan, especially if there are fewer disruptions, referrals to the principal, and test scores are improving. Use data to show the correlation between improved social behavior and academic achievement.

Be prepared to handle as much discipline within the classroom as possible. Speak with the vice-principal, if your school has one, to see if you can find a sympathetic advocate in that position. If you happen to be an acquaintance with the president of the PTA or PTO, sound that person out to see if he or she is concerned about bullying. Try to build a network. Don't forget the power of The Law of the Few.

#8 "Why aren't punishments for bullies harsher? Why are the targets the ones who have to change schools?"

It is very unjust that many families whose children are being bullied bear the greatest burden by moving or transferring their child away from the abusive school situation. Sometimes they turn to home schooling.

A recent study released by the U.S. Department of Education estimates that as of 2007, 1.5 million children or 2.9 percent of all school-age children are being educated at home, up from 850,000 in 1999. *USA Today* released the data in an article in May 2009. A significant shift occurred in the ratio of girls being home schooled. In 1999, it was 49 percent boys, 51 percent girls. Currently girls represent 58 percent compared to 42 percent of boys. There is speculation that mean-girl bullying is an underlying reason. In fact, 21 percent of parents cited concerns about the school environment while 17 percent cited dissatisfaction with academic instruction. To provide religious or moral instruction was identified by 36 percent of parents.

Parents who are willing to challenge the school hierarchy and succeed in their demands must be persistent and realize that it will take a great deal of patience and fortitude. When all else fails, some parents have taken the legal route and been victorious, but it can be extremely expensive and very time-consuming.

As for harsher penalties for bulliers, again and again we come back to prevention and intervention at the earliest possible stage of a child's development. When do we give up on a youngster who never had a caring adult who believed in his or her worth?

Data gathered in the National Pre-kindergarten Study (NPS) presents expulsion data from all forty states that fund pre-kindergarten programs. In classrooms where teachers had no access to psychologists or psychiatrists, 10.8 pre-kindergartners per one thousand were expelled. If we are expelling pre-kindergartners, what is this saying about our ability to manage unruly children? And what kinds of interventions were used before expulsion?

What kind of discipline is most effective? Our harshest punishment is expulsion but how can we congratulate ourselves when we remove an incorrigible bullier from our school and throw him or her into our neighborhood and our community with no supervision to inflict even greater harm on more people?

Alternative schools can be an answer for many young people. Extremely aggressive children must be held accountable, and placed in a setting that can deal with their issues. The targets stay in their familiar surroundings and the young perpetrators are given a second chance. There are exemplary models of alternative schools, which have turned many young people's lives around. In smaller communities where alternative schools are not available, regional residential treatment facilities might serve their needs. The next step, unfortunately, is prison. One out of every ninety-nine persons in the United States is in prison. What happened, or didn't happen to those inmates when they were in school?

Even the juvenile justice system is moving toward rehabilitation in small groups, constant therapeutic interventions, and minimal force. They are moving away from control that is maintained through incarceration, coercion, and punishment. The Missouri Division of Youth Services is a prime example of such a promising reform movement that is being emulated by other states. Humane facilities are organized into groups of ten to twelve young people who do everything together, including daily chores, school, activities, and group sessions. Physical and emotional safety is maintained through structure, supervision, relationships, and group process. When a conflict or concern arises, a group circle is called by any group member or staff. The agency's director, Tim Decker, describes the process: "when a circle-up is called, everyone stops what they are doing to share observations, feelings, discuss alternatives, and help each other achieve their goals." Youth and staff safety is increased because of the empathy, camaraderie, and trust that occurs. In traditional youth corrections programs, youth are four and a half times and staff are thirteen times more likely to be assaulted and injured than they are in Missouri. This data is from Dick Mendel's research in the 2010 Annie E. Casey Report on the Missouri Division of Youth services.

If these methods are working with young men and women who have become part of the criminal population, why can't we use them with students who haven't reached that stage?

#9 "How do I handle a bully whose parent is the principal or superintendent or a member of the School Board?"

Chances are the child has been given a free ride for much too long because of the parent's status. The child has paid a serious price for the deferential treatment. From the moment that son or daughter enters your classroom, he or she must be treated exactly the same as all other students and expectations for appropriate behavior never lowered. That will be in the best interest of the student, the best interest of the classmates, and in the long run, the best interest of the parent.

Request a parent conference with the principal and guide the conversation the same as in dealing with a parent in question #1. You might be the one person who is capable of administering the "tough love," the firm hand the child desperately needs. If the principal challenges you, respond by saying you assumed that you would be expected to honor the school Code of Conduct for all students, as you have always done. Document every entanglement you have with the student and the principal in detail. Contact the president of the Teacher's Union when trouble first starts brewing and alert that person to a possible problem. Hold to your standards and work diligently not to become adversarial with the principal. This is where past performance will serve you well.

#10 "What is the best way for me to approach the classroom about bullying?"

The best way is to have a discussion about bullying prevention at the beginning of the year, before bullying occurs. Once situations have erupted and children have become identified as bulliers and/or targets, the discussion won't seem as generic. Speak openly and honestly about expectations. Believe, profoundly, that bullying is not normal, inevitable behavior. Here are five strategies:

1) Focus on Positive Behavior

Remember Mrs. Gardner, who at the very beginning of the semester told her students that her highest priority was for students to treat each other with respect and dignity. Mrs. Gardner emphasized that: "We need this room to feel completely safe so you can learn as much as possible." Talk about the classroom being a bully-free zone. Recognize support and kindness whenever it occurs. Affirming prosocial interactions can accomplish wonders.

2) Identify Bullying Situations

Encourage witnesses to report bullying situations to you and assure them of confidentiality. Explain that the more students who give information, there is less likelihood for retaliation. Be vigilant for every sign of cruelty. Be on high alert for indications of shunning or ostracizing. Remember that the sooner intervention takes place, the greater opportunity for resolution will take place.

3) Make the Issue Interesting

Engage students by seeking out powerful DVDs on the topic; bring in an outside speaker who will reinforce your approach. Find ways to connect bullying issues to various subjects—English, Math, Social Studies, and so on. English lessons can easily be connected to captivating literature, books, and stories about bullying. Social studies can include the frequent newspaper articles that appear about bullying, or even better, about people who make a difference in other people's lives.

Math could be an opportunity to use the social norm approach and survey the class about their perceptions of student attitudes about bullying. Check out the National Center for Social Norming for survey questions. Have students estimate what percentage believe students treat each other respectfully, what percentage believe that students have the right to feel safe, what percentage believe that students will support classmates who are being bullied. After the surveys have been turned in, have the class compile the perceptions and compare them with the class averages.

Above all, model the behavior you want your students to exhibit and affirm individual and classroom exemplary behavior. Be the thermostat to set the tone.

13

Parents as Protectors, Partners, and Change Agents

"The hardest part of being a parent is when your child is being bullied at school."

—Martin, a parent

PARENTS AS PROTECTORS

Parent of a Target

How will you know if your child is being bullied? If your child continually finds excuses not to go to school, that is a major clue. If your child's behavior changes dramatically by becoming aggressive or withdrawn, that is another indication.

The best, of course, will be if your child confides in you. Many children will not report to their parents that they are being bullied. They are reluctant to confess that they have become a target because they think they should be able to take care of bullying problems themselves. They don't want to risk losing your approval. Other children are concerned that their parents will get too upset and do something to make the situation worse. Lastly, they fear that you will dismiss what they have to say and do nothing to protect them.

If you are fortunate enough that your child reports to you they are being bullied, accept that report as a gift. Children trust you to be a Protector. Telling them to ignore the bullier is most likely a tactic they have tried before they came to you. They deserve a more sophisticated response. Let your child know that bullying is serious and you will be there to support them until the bullying stops.

Physical and Verbal Bullying
Plan A should be to empower your children to resolve the situation themselves. Begin by asking questions and document everything you learn. Write

down names, dates, places, and the types of bullying they describe, which you might need in the future.

Questions should include: "When and where does the bullying occur most often?" "What is the form of bullying—physical, verbal, emotional, gender, cyber?" "What student or students are involved?" "Are there any other students present?" "Are there any adults who are aware of what is happening to you?" "Is there more than one bullier?" "How have you responded?" "Has it ever worked?" "Does the student(s) who is bullying you pick on others as well?" "How do other students deal with the bullier?" "Have you ever seen someone else handle the bullier successfully?" "What did they do or say?" "Have you had an idea that you haven't tried yet?" "What if we role play?" "You be the bullier and I'll be you."

Role-playing has helped many students by having a script they could practice with their parents. It's difficult to come up with zingers when you're in the throes of pain, but if you can rehearse some lines in advance, it's easier to deflect the situation in the moment.

We talk to students about the difference between a passive response, an aggressive response, and an assertive response. For instance, if someone says: "Your hair is so ugly," a passive response would be to internalize the put-down and be ashamed of your hair. An aggressive response would be to retort with: "Well, my hair may be ugly, but it's not nearly as ugly as your face." Now, *you* have become the bullier!

There are numerous possibilities for an assertive response. "When I looked in the mirror this morning, I had the very same thought—I am having a really bad hair day," or "You have such terrific hair. You are so lucky, I sure wish I had hair like you!" or "Thank you for noticing my hair problem, do you have a suggestion for a stylist (or barber)?" or "How would you feel if someone said that to you?" or "What's going on with you that you have a need to do this?" Many students have learned to say "So?" or "Thank you" or "Have a good day."

There is a marvelous little book by Alice Cohen-Posey, *How to Handle Bullies, Teasers, & Other Meanies* (1995), that gives excellent suggestions for come-backs and one-liners. Get a copy and use it to find a phrase that feels comfortable for your child.

Some children just can't muster the nerve to respond verbally to their tormentor. If that is the case, nonverbal strategies need to be in your child's repertoire. Body language can reveal obvious cues that reward bullies. To make the point we tell children: "When you lower your chin, the bulliers win. When you lift your chin, then you can win." One parent helped her son by giving him the imagery of a suit of armor. She suggested that he imagine himself wearing a protective metal shield to deflect all of the verbal barbs. She even went to a costume shop and bought him one to wear around the house to practice feeling invincible—and it worked!

We recommend that you expose your child to the martial arts such as karate, tae kwon do, or tai chi. We have heard wonderful reports from parents whose children blossomed when they experienced the centering and respect that are part of these eastern forms of movement. Posture is a noticeable feature that signals strength or vulnerability to a bullier.

If you can convince your son or daughter that bulliers are the ones with the problem, not them, you will have made real headway. Ask your child what he or she suspects is the reason why the student is bullying. A child psychiatrist, Dr. Richard Davis, found that parents were amazed at how quickly the bullying problem could be solved when the target child gives up the self-blame that accompanies bullying. When children who have failed to stand up for themselves become confident enough to take control, their problem can be solved directly.

A thoughtful young boy at Scarsdale Middle School shared his personal epiphany. He told us that all through elementary school, where he was a favorite target, he tried to pretend that he wasn't bothered, but his body betrayed his vulnerability. The summer before he attended middle school, something happened that he couldn't explain. "I grew myself up inside." When he started sixth grade, he didn't have to pretend how he felt, because he just didn't care how the bulliers behaved. "I decided that I was going to be in charge of who I was, not someone else." The bullying ceased.

Explain to your child how powerful it makes bulliers feel if they can incite you to cry.

Tears give bullies enormous satisfaction. Tears are a normal response to a painful predicament, but if there is any way your child can postpone the tears until reaching the bathroom at school or his or her bedroom at home, it will deny bulliers the sense of power they crave.

Humor has been a magical solution for many students. Nothing takes the steam out of a bullier's tirade like a joke. One boy shared his formula for success. He kept making the bullier laugh, until his tormentor relinquished his jibes and became his friend instead.

Storytelling is an excellent tool. Children love to hear stories from your youth. Share incidents that occurred when you were their age. Knowing that you once struggled with hurtful peers and now you have become this strong, capable, caring adult is inspiring, to say the least.

Emotional Bullying

The strategies for dealing with the nonverbal manifestations of emotional bullying—such as making faces, pointing, staring, flicking someone off, hand signs, snickering, drawing pictures, writing notes, are the same as suggested for physical and verbal. But when bullying comes in the form of psychological abuse—such as rejection, isolation, exclusion, and/or ostracizing, new coping skills must come into play.

James Garbarino, in his book, *See Jane Hit: Why Girls Are Growing More Violent and What We Can Do about It* (2006), claims that "Human beings are social creatures and to feel right about themselves they need to be in relationships. This seems to be particularly true of girls, who tend to be more affiliative than boys."

The arc of female gossip and rumor spreading can reach horrific proportions, but the withdrawal of contact can be absolutely devastating. Sometimes girls drift apart as their new interest in boys attracts like-minded friends. The kind of meanness that singles someone out for isolation, that is intentional and often without apparent reason, is in a category of its own. How can a girl respond assertively to a clique of girls who were her friends on Tuesday, but will have nothing to do with her on Wednesday? In addition to abandonment, girls will resort to cyberbullying to plot a full-scale orchestration of exclusion. Though girls have finely honed their expertise in this category of rejection, boys are not exempt from isolation from their peer group.

Our advice for parents on this particular form of bullying is complex. You can demand that someone stop hitting your child, but how can you demand that someone accept and include your child as a friend?

Encourage your daughter or son to find a friend or group of friends outside of school. Perhaps a youth group, a dancing class, a chess club, or a community service project will open up new connections. Help your child develop a talent, a passion for an interest, a focus on an idea that's worthy of pursuit. A pet that offers unconditional love can make a tremendous difference. One friend, one trustworthy friend, can be life-changing.

A fascinating Australian study on friendship found that older people with a large circle of friends were 22 percent less likely to die during the study period than those with fewer friends. In the same *New York Times* article (2009) written by Tara Parker-Pope, Harvard researchers reported that strong social ties could promote brain health. Rebecca G. Adams, a professor of sociology at the University of North Carolina, Greensboro, claims that "Friendship has a bigger impact on our psychological well-being than family relationships." These and other studies corroborate the fact that friendship has a profound psychological effect. This information underscores the need for parents to add friendships to their "must do" list for their children.

Above all, tell your child that bulliers' motives are most probably unfathomable and dwelling on how to regain their favor will not be fruitful. Moving forward with a strong sense of self and personal resolve will do more to diminish their power than anything else.

Ask your child's permission to talk to the school counselor who may have some ideas to engage your daughter or son in a project with another student in need of a friend. Maybe he or she could tutor a younger student or a special-ed youngster who needs some extra attention.

Reassure your child of their virtues, authentic attributes they can accept as true. Do not shower them with pity but rather search with them for a workable result.

Sexual Bullying

Sexual harassment is a form of discrimination prohibited by Title VII of the Civil Rights Act of 1964 and Title IX of the Education Amendments of 1972. Sexual harassment is a term familiar to children but usually empty of definition. The legal definition consists of unwelcome sexual advances, requests for sexual favors, sexually motivated physical conduct, or other verbal or physical conduct or communication.

Be sure to document any infraction with date, place, and time. Your children will be more likely to report any harassment to you if you had previous frank and open sexual conversations with your daughters and your sons. If they sense you are uncomfortable about the subject, they will protect your discomfort.

Cyberbullying

The National Crime Prevention Council has an excellent website with excellent information and recommendations—www.ncpc.org. Some of the recommendations include having an important discussion with your teens about the risks. Keep communication open so they will trust you with any cyberbullying they experience. Advise your teens never to post or share personal information online and to refuse to pass along cyberbullying messages to others.

Monitor your teen's use of the computer by installing it in a central location where you can have access. Learn how to block cyberbullying messages through your Internet service provider, social network site, or chat room moderator. If your teen is being cyberbullied, be sure to save the evidence that you may need for reporting purposes.

A good example of a Parent as Protector is a father who insisted that his son include him as a "friend" on his Facebook site. The father checks to see what websites his son is exploring, scrutinizes his Facebook page and randomly checks his son's cell phone messages. Some may find these methods intrusive but parents today must become savvy about preventing or at least intervening in the savagery and recklessness that has become commonplace with cyberbullying. Formspring is a more recent site and is viewed by some as a more treacherous social media form of communication.

In your role as Protector, be reminded that Plan A was to empower your child to manage his or her own problem—no matter which form of bullying. In spite of all your efforts, this doesn't always work. Plan B could be contacting the parent of the bullier or the bullier directly. Many experts warn against such action. There are some notable risks that we will spell out.

Before you contact the parent of the bullier, keep in mind that some child bulliers are the product of a home where bullying is the norm. Such a parent might support their child's behavior, indeed they may have instructed the child to be tough, not to show any signs of weakness, and to strike first to avoid being on the defensive. That same parent may try to intimidate you and cause you to lose your calm demeanor. The parent may inform the bullier of your call. Either of these responses could make the situation worse.

At parent seminars, when this question of strategy emerges, parents always say they would want to know if their child is bullying. On several occasions, parents have volunteered how embarrassing it was to have the school identify their child as a bullier to another child when the parent of the target is a friend of theirs. If you think your friend would prefer to hear about the problem from you, practice your approach and try it out with a spouse or neighbor before you try it out with your friend.

Several creative parents have described how they solved the bullying problem with other parents. One parent invited the family of the bullier, including the offender, to a picnic supper. The parents made a pleasant connection and continued socializing with their children in hand. As designed, the family relationship neutralized the tormenting.

A father told of being furious about the abuse his son was experiencing at the hand of an extremely cruel boy. The father marched up to school, demanding that the offender be expelled, only to learn that the bullier had recently lost his father in a tragic automobile accident and had been on a rampage against everyone ever since. The father of the target went home and invited the bullier to go on a fishing trip the next weekend with him and his son.

A number of mothers and fathers have confronted the bulliers of their children directly and forcefully, at school and outside of school successfully. Consider many options, just as your child needs to do.

Plan C involves contacting the school. Assume that the school is your ally and will take responsible action. Start by contacting the teacher. If, for some reason, the teacher is not responsive, call the counselor, then the vice-principal, the principal, the superintendent—all the way up the ladder until someone takes responsibility to stop the bullying. No matter how upset you are, get your feelings under control and handle every encounter in a respectful way. Accusations tend to make people defensive. Be appreciative of support. Be sure to keep your documentation current, including the nonresponses of any staff you contact.

If that chain of command doesn't bring results, contact the school board and as a last resort, consider engaging a lawyer. Your child needs to appreciate that you will not cease to pursue accountability until the bullying stops. Many parents have given up on their school system and enrolled their child in a different school or chosen to home school their student.

If your child does not report any bullying situations to you, as a Protector, you must still be alert for any indication that bullying is taking place. At the beginning of this chapter we listed some informative clues. If you notice any behavior changes or excuses to avoid school, initiate a calm conversation with your child. If information isn't forthcoming, a visit to your child's doctor might be in order. Share your suspicions and concerns in advance of the appointment.

Parent of a Bullier

Many parents have been shocked to learn that their child who had never been linked with physical, verbal, emotional, or gender/sexual bullying has found cyberbullying to be very seductive. The technological anonymity unleashes behaviors that had been previously unthinkable. Because most parents have not been exposed to the power of cruelty that students inflict through texting, Myspace, Facebook, cellphones, and so on, you may be completely unaware of your child's involvement. It is imperative to have a discussion about this pervasive form of bullying and insist that communication you would not dare to make in person is off limits via technology.

What if your child is a bullier? Get your emotions under control. Ask yourself a series of demanding questions: Is your child under a lot of stress? Has he or she joined a new group of friends who act out aggressively? Has some great disappointment or frustration left a residue of unresolved anger? Could your child have been a target and has resorted to bullying as a self-defense technique? Has he or she decided that being aggressive is the only way to survive the schoolyard battlefield? Could your child be imitating behaviors from home or from pop culture? Is bullying a parenting style? Is there any sibling abuse occurring? An inquiring, constructive conversation is in order. Determining the root of the bullying behavior is your goal. Begin by citing the qualities you admire in your child and expressing concern about behavior that is out of character, if this is, in truth, the case. You want your child to believe that you have his or her best interest at heart. This dialogue should not be judgmental, but one of information gathering. You will need good communication skills to make this work and being critical at this point will not be helpful. This is a good time to practice your own empathy skills and put yourself inside your child's being. If our behavior is a response to our thought process, it's imperative to get through to your son's or daughter's thought process. Once you discover why they are engaging in bullying behavior, you can devise a thoughtful reaction.

Don't attempt to uncover the problem and solve it in the same conversation. Give yourself some time to digest what you have learned. Getting feedback from another family member could be very valuable. Never be reluctant to reach out for professional assistance if you feel stymied.

Sometimes it's the family culture that needs dissecting. Elizabeth Sweeney found increasing evidence of a family connection with bullying. She reviewed research from England, Germany, Norway, Japan, South Africa, and the United States primarily involving children between the ages of nine and sixteen. In her findings, published August 2008, she reported that "children raised by authoritarian parents—parents who are demanding, directive, and unresponsive—are the most prone to act out bullying behavior."

She also wrote that "children who experience hostility, abuse, physical discipline and other aggressive behaviors by their parents are more likely to model that behavior in their peer relationships. Children learn from their parents how to behave and interact with others. If they're learning about aggression and angry words at home, they will tend to use these behaviors as coping mechanisms when they interact with peers."

On the flip side are the parents of bulliers who are caring, loving, and nurturing. They don't understand their children's antisocial behavior and are at their wits end, desperate for help. They are losing control of their children and they are in constant conflict with them at home over a broad range of antisocial behavior, including bullying.

Key findings of the Bale report published by the not-for-profit Parentline Plus in the United Kingdom in 2004 were based on nine hundred calls to their twenty-four-hour free helpline. "Eighty percent of the parents talked about high levels of conflict with their child, 69 percent spoke about their child's high level of anger, and 77 percent reported that their child was having problems at school, with more than half saying that their child had been excluded or was playing truant."

Parents of bulliers were three times more likely to report that their child was lying and twice as likely to mention stealing, smoking, and drug abuse. Conflict with peers was another concern, with 20 percent talking about their children being in with a bad crowd." One typical parent called in reporting that she and her husband were "at the end of their tether" concerning their fifteen-year-old daughter who was engaged in underage sex, bullying behavior at school, and who was verbally abusive at home.

Don Braun, the chief executive of Parentline Plus said, "These findings concern us greatly. Not only are parents of bulliers telling us they are losing control, but the statistics demonstrate the very high levels of conflict both within the families, the school, and the community. It is essential that when schools and communities develop policies to cut down on bullying and to ensure community safety, the families of bulliers are recognized as needing responsive and appropriate help with their family life, and not further isolation."

Our advice for parents of younger children or children who still respect your authority is to be proactive in your relationship with them. Mobilize their feelings of empathy and/or reduce their stress. It will be easier to get in touch with the thought process of a younger child and to set limits and impose boundaries and consequences for unacceptable behaviors. Limit the time your child spends engaged in video games, TV, music, or movies with violent content.

Let your children know that you care about their needs but you will not allow them to cause pain for someone else. Do not become an enabler.

Here is a checklist for parents to think about. Does your child get pleasure from taunting others; enjoy spreading rumors; seek power and control over others; act out anger by hitting, kicking, damaging property; play on others' insecurity; use words to humiliate or ridicule others; refuse to admit mistakes and correct them; have serious problems with siblings; witness abusive behavior in your home; lack a sense of humor; lack empathy; find it pleasurable to torture animals?

If you can be brutally honest and see a pattern of your child's behavior in this checklist, you are on a constructive path for change. If you find yourself in a state of constant irritation and frustration, consider professional help.

Speak with personnel in your child's school. Inform them about the steps you have taken and find out how you could work together to bring about a change in attitude. School personnel will respect you for recognizing the situation and will make a special effort to cooperate. The earlier you confront the problem, the sooner it can become resolved.

Parent of a Witness

Most likely, your child has been a witness. There might be some exceptions, but for the most part, every child is an observer of some form of peer abuse. Witnessing bullying without being a participant does not leave a child unscathed. In chapter 2 we highlighted the role of the witness and made recommendations for educators. In this chapter, we want to pinpoint the parent's role.

Encourage your child to take some action to support a target, such as not becoming an audience for a bullier or laugh at the bullier's put-downs. Talk to your child about connecting with a positive peer group that won't join forces with a bullier for self-protection.

Have a conversation about the difference between tattling and reporting and remind them that reporting is being responsible. Keep communication going and inquire from time to time if they have found a way to reach out to a target who is in need of support.

Model good witness behavior. Paula Fried, co-author of *Bullies, Targets, & Witnesses* (2003), described a situation she witnessed when picking up her son from school. She was lined up with all of the other mothers in their vans at curbside when two boys ran out of school, threw their books on the ground, and started beating on each other. Paula looked to see if anyone was rushing to their rescue but no such hero appeared. She looked at all of the other mothers who were frozen in their driver's seats and made the decision to intervene.

She strode forcefully to the boys and calmly suggested that they find some other way to settle their dispute. They looked at her quizzically, gathered up their books, and left the scene. Paula returned to her car, only to notice that the two boys were now at the street corner, books scattered and exchanging blows. Once again, she walked determinedly to the site of the altercation and tried to reason with the boys about their fighting. Once again, the boys gathered their belongings and this time fled out of sight.

Paula is firmly convinced that her efforts had no effect on "stopping the fight" and that they renewed their punches at some location beyond view. What she did realize was that numerous adults witnessed two boys lashing out at each other but either felt helpless or chose not to intercede. If nothing else, she set an example for responsible witness behavior.

PARENTS AS PARTNERS

If you want to be a solid partner with your school, become the best parent that you can be. In this section, we have gathered helpful research and data for parents who want their children's educational years to be satisfying and successful.

Beginning at birth, take advantage of two extraordinary programs that support new families, if they are available in your community. Parents as Teachers offers its services to any new family, and Healthy Families America provides services for parents who need more intense contact. A trained parent educator will work with you during your child's first three years of life. The Parent Educator or Home Visitor serves as a caring coach whose intent is to support you to become the best parent possible.

The American Academy of Pediatrics says children under the age of two shouldn't watch TV at all and that older kids should watch no more than two hours a day. While there is a great deal of conflicting data about media influence, there's little disagreement that violent programs are bad for children, leading to fear and aggressive behavior and that TV in a child's bedroom can lead to sleep disorders.

Be sure to give your children the basic social skills to prepare them for the school socializing experience. By the time children enter kindergarten they should know how to share, how to treat adults with respect, to master basic manners and etiquette, to have a good sense of right and wrong, and how to be kind. Your children will develop and absorb more basic information in the first three to five years of their lives than in any other comparable time period. Before your children ever appear at the school door, your influence on their behavior is firmly imprinted.

Children who feel respected will in turn respect others. The more control they exert over their own actions, the less likely they will need to control others. When you love your children unconditionally and consistently, the sense of security they will receive is priceless.

Teaching children to manage their anger is a critical task of parenting. Families in particular and society in general need to find better ways to deal with the anger and rage. Driving habits have cost people their lives and "road rage" has entered our vocabulary. Children need to learn how to express anger appropriately, to calm down when they're ready to explode, and to handle their frustrations and disappointments in healthy ways.

The ability to develop impulse control has surprising power to predict a child's future. "The marshmallow test" which consists of challenging a four-year-old to sit at a table with a marshmallow. If the child can wait until an adult comes in the room, the child will get two marshmallows. If the child can't wait that long, he or she just gets the one.

An article in the *Boston Globe* by Carey Goldberg states that the longer the child can hold back, from a minute to twenty minutes, the better the outlook in later life for everything from SAT scores to social skills to academic achievement. Columbia University psychologist Walter Mischel has followed his test subjects from preschool in the late 1960s into their forties now. The ability to delay gratification truly correlates with success in life, according to the research. The fascinating study appeared in the September 1989 edition of *Psychological Science*. There are training techniques that are worth parental curiosity.

Resilience is a topic that has been heavily researched. Emmy E. Werner and Ruth Smith conducted a thirty-year study that found identifiable factors that build resilience. Having an adult mentor is the most significant.

Effective reading skills by age eight was one of the most potent predictors of successful adult adaptation. Children who were given responsibilities, especially looking out for the welfare of others, fared well. Werner and Smith discovered that social skills advanced popularity, and popular children have more friends, are more confident, cheerful, humorous, and intelligent.

Resilient children know how to find and use information to solve problems. When faced with adversity, they look at many options to deal with their circumstance. Hobbies and interests bring children in contact with more people who can bring comfort and solace in times of stress. Finally, resilient children have hope and plans for the future.

Putting practices in place to help your children develop resiliency will certainly come in handy when bullying situations crop up.

One thing is clear: however you deal with your own emotions when you are distressed, angry, or frustrated will surely be copied by your offspring. As always, being a role model is the most persuasive lecture you will ever give.

Always assume that you are a partner with your children's teachers in their school success. You and the classroom teacher are a double dose of education and protection. No one else will spend more time with your child or understand their triumphs and their quirks. You see your child in the context of your family; the teacher sees your child in the context of a class of fifteen to thirty children, not to mention the years of working with countless other children of the same age. Their observations about your child should be received openly, even when you are learning things unpleasant to hear.

We must acknowledge that there are teachers who are negligent about dealing with bullying situations and even teachers who are bullies themselves. Begin with the teacher, even when unresponsive, and document the failed conversation. Then follow the chain of command.

There is one last stipulation to being a valuable partner with your school. It has to do with the computer. There is universal agreement that children should not have a computer in their bedroom. The extent of tragic electronic bullying has led to unanimous calls for parents to monitor the Internet communication in their home. Parents cannot expect schools to be wholly responsible for the transgressions of their children—anytime, anywhere. As one thoughtful lawyer observed, would we expect the school to be responsible for a fight that occurred between your child and a neighbor in your front yard? At what point should the school be expected to control all damaging behaviors between peers?

PARENTS AS ADVOCATES

Parents can be extremely effective advocates, not only for their own children but for other children as well. You can become involved with your PTA/PTO to make antibullying a year-long priority. You can make the same commitment to your Girl Scout, Boy Scout, Campfire, and/or other youth groups. These organizations have access to quality materials, programs, and activities about bullying. Girl Scouts of America has created wonderful resources and sponsored national workshops on bullying prevention. Offer to pay for a qualified speaker to come to your school or weekly meeting or camp. Your support may make the difference in a child's life.

Make your carpool a No Put-Down Zone. Explain to all of your passengers that there will be no name-calling or rudeness while you are the driver. Share with them how important it is to you that everyone feels physically and emotionally safe when you are their driver.

Make the same rules for sleepovers at your home. No sabotage. One mother learned that her daughter, Trisha, was being invited to a pajama party where some of the girls were going to be subjected to humiliation. The hostess and some of her friends were going to tie their guests' clothing in knots and put their bras in the freezer. Trisha's mom contacted the mother of the hostess and disclosed the plot. The sleepover was cancelled. Initially, Trisha was furious at her mother for interfering. A few of the girls retaliated by shunning Trisha. Ultimately, Trisha realized that she was going to be the brunt of their dirty tricks, one way or the other.

Sports are ripe for bullying. We have been horrified to read about parents who were responsible for the death of an ice-hockey coach or another parent because of their fury about a decision during a game—adult role modeling gone amok.

You will have countless opportunities to discuss the art of winning and losing with your children and to bring reason to Bleacher Behavior.

One of our favorite stories is the case of a young boy, Ernie, who was uncoordinated and rather nonathletic. Despite his liabilities, he enjoyed playing soccer and his coach believed that sports were not just about competition. He believed there were skills to be learned—such as teamwork, self-discipline, giving your very best. Every player was given an equal chance to play during the game, regardless of his ability. The parents were thrilled to have a coach with such solid values. That is, everyone but Ernie's dad, Sonny.

Sonny showed up at every game, that was the good news. The bad news was that whenever Ernie was rotated in and missed a kick, his father stood up in the stands and screamed at him for being "such a slug." "Can't you ever do anything right?" "Stop rushing the ball!" Ernie was mortified and the other parents were in agony. They were embarrassed for Ernie and angry at his father but felt helpless to change the situation. They got together and decided not to confront the father, fearing it would make him even more belligerent. Instead, whenever Ernie came on the field, all of the parents cheered him on. They drowned out his father with words of encouragement—"Hang in there, Ernie," "You're doing your best," "Keep trying!" That is parent advocacy at its very best.

Become familiar with your school Code of Conduct for staff and students. Many schools insist that students and parents read and sign the Code of Conduct. Your School Board should have an antibullying policy and your state should have pertinent legislation. Forty-five states have passed antibullying laws and those laws have been rated by an energetic agency, www.bullypolice.com. Check out the legislation that exists or does not exist in your state. If your state is one that does not have antibullying legislation, contact BullyPoliceUSA. They have constructive strategies to offer and will coach you on how to maximize your involvement.

Parent Meeting on Bullying Prevention

Make a special effort to attend any PTA or PTO meetings on the topic of bullying or school safety. Attendance is usually confined to a small group of parents of the targets and the officers of the parent organization. Changing the school culture cannot be borne by those who are in pain, alone. One of your children may have a solid social standing but the next one might not. Make a commitment to the ideals of the school community, regardless of the comfort level of your current student.

Offer to be part of a Planning Committee to capture a wider audience. Recruit a group of fathers to perform a "Kindness Rap" at the PTA/PTO Bullying Meeting, with appropriate baseball caps on backward, et al. Ask the principal to assign the Student Council to conduct a school survey about bullying issues and give a report of their findings at the meeting. Offer to be part of the Hospitality Committee who will serve supper or dessert at the event.

Volunteer to assist with recess and/or supervise bus rides on field trips. It will mean a great deal to your sons and daughters and be an enormous boon to the teachers and bus drivers. Be sure to enforce the situational rules.

It is the responsibility of parents to teach manners and etiquette to their children. Basic concepts of respect, courtesy, "please," "may I," "thank you," and "pardon me," should be instilled in your children before they ever attend school. A conversation with a teacher who was dealing with an influx of children who had escaped the devastation of Hurricane Katrina in New Orleans was very informative. She had made an assumption that integrating those students into her classroom was going to be a tremendous chore. To her great surprise, the children always answered her questions with "Yes, ma'am and No ma'am." The gift of politeness enriched all of her students and made learning easier for everyone.

You may not realize that your child is bullying. Listen with an open mind to information that school staff shares with you. Support school polices on antibullying behavior and reinforce those adopted codes of conduct in your own home.

Consider yourself a valuable link in the chain of Change Agents who believe that change is possible and are passionate about the outcome. Joanne Stern, in her book *Parenting Is a Contact Sport: 8 Ways to Stay Connected to Your Kids for Life* (2009), gives us wonderful advice—"Build a relationship with your children that's so strong, nothing will sever it. From toddlerhood to teen years and beyond, you can make 'real' contact with your kids, forming an unbreakable bond that makes you the person they want to share with and gives you the opportunity to guide and counsel them in every phase of their lives."

14

Letters from Children

"The greatest revenge is not to defend the enemy but to change his heart."

—Author Unknown

Our final plea is for children's pain to be listened to with respect and a sense of urgency. In this chapter we are including a small sample of the thousands of letters that we have received. Some wrote as bulliers, some as targets, some as witnesses, some from multiple roles. The pain that is taking place is staggering. We see it in the eyes of the children, their teachers, their principals, their counselors, and their parents. We share their frustration, their heartache, and their tears. We must find a way to stop the pain!

BULLIES

by Teegan Fifield

What is a bully? A person who picks on someone? Well, yeah, that's true, but a bully is also much more.

I was in kindergarten, eating glue, and yelling at my teacher and classmates. That's why I got sent to the principal's office for the first time. I'll never forget the fear that soon turned to pride, as I walked into the principal's office. I was proud, proud to have people fear me.

Through the years the principal's office became my second home. I got in many fights with the boys my age. I soon got used to teachers yelling at me and filling our plans and detentions. Right after seventh grade started I realized that being a bully wasn't what I wanted for my life. I wanted to have friends, no enemies. So I began to change. It was a slow process, changing the way I acted, the only way I knew.

Starting eighth grade I promised myself that this year would be different. This was the year I'd make a difference. This was the year, my year to free myself and become a new person.

Well, I'm sad to say that right off I began on people. This continued on and on until one day something changed my life. The author, SuEllen Fried, came to talk to the eighth grade. She talked to us about why people are bullies. During the assembly I sat back and really took a look at my life and the lives of those around me. I realized that I really was a bully. I've never felt more shame than I felt that day. I decided that I had to change before I really messed up.

So I started to change right then, with an apology to a friend whom I had hurt so deeply. I never knew such little words as "I'm sorry" could change so many things and help so much. I'm on a search to find the real me, someone I'm not sure I'll ever find. I never knew what an impact each one of us has on life until I really looked. I wasted so many years being a bully instead of being nice. I've definitely learned my lesson. And although I'm trying, I will never be the "perfect angel" by far. I admit that I have a bad temper, but I'm working on it.

To all the bullies out there, it's not worth it. You can't judge people by their differences because that's what makes them who they are.

The following letters are printed, unedited, as they were received, without the students' names.

LETTER #1

Last year, my handicapped brother and I went to the pool and people would talk about my brother. They weren't comments—they were bad things like "retard" and "idiot." This wasn't funny. It was verbal bullying on him and emotional bullying on both of us. I am 100 percent sure he didn't like it. I know I hated it. I told them to shut up, he's not a retard, he's my brother. Then they would stop. I'm sure they would make fun of him when I'm not around.

I was embarrassed. I thought people would be nice to him. There are a lot, but some people would be jerks. He had people stick up to him. They got to know him and then they stopped. I was happy!

So my brother told the lifeguards and if they saw anyone bully him they made them Stop and sit out. So it isn't nice to make of the special needs. It is very, very mean.

LETTER #2

When I was in the 4th grade, I would walk into class late. I was called names, they laughed as they pointed at me. When we went outside for recess the best thing to do was to play kickball. When I would ask if I could play they either looked away or said "No." There was not just one person that would pick on me, it was all of the kids. They made fun of me because of my hair, clothing and shoes, my whole life. By the 7th grade I was tired of everyone picking on me. I sometimes told my mom that I was sick and that I could not go to school. I was never sick, I just said that so that I would not have to go to school.

There was no sexual or physical bullying. They would point at me and laugh and they would yell untrue things about me during class. I felt that none of my classmates liked me too much.

In 6th grade it didn't happen as much as it did in 4th and 5th grade. In 4th and 5th grade it was something that happened to me every day. In 6th grade the same thing happened but not as much. I never got F's on my report card but sometimes I got D's. Then in front of the whole class they would yell out what I got. The thing that really burned me was that the teacher never did anything.

In the beginning of 7th grade there was a girl by the name of Shannon. She was popular and that surprised me that she reached out to me. She would let me eat with them at lunch and at recess she would let me play kickball with them. Since that day I will never forget what she did for me. I still hang out with her and a lot of other people, too.

I still know that people talk about me behind my back, but now it doesn't bother me as much as it used to. Shannon has helped me out with a lot of things in my life.

LETTER #3

I know this kid in my grade that gets picked on all the time. People call him names and call him gay, faggot, and homo. I feel sorry for him because it happens every day.

Last year people started making fun of him when he would take a shower for basketball. They started nasty rumors and he felt terrible. Sometimes people make him so mad that he starts fights with them. When he first moved here, no one liked him. He got beat up all the time. I see people just go up and punch him for no reason and just laugh. He would come to school the next day with bruises all over his arm. Just a couple of nights ago, people held him down and punched him in the chest and kicked him in the balls.

I hope people stop picking on him soon. It isn't funny and I don't think they would like it if he did it to them.

LETTER #4

Most people picture the perfect bully as a male, oversized person picking on or hurting people that are different or smaller than themselves. They have a high self-esteem when it comes to anything kids say or do to them. It seems that everything they do is right and everybody is scared of them so nobody mouths off or does anything back to them. This theory is not always true, at least not the part about being male and oversized. Come to think of it most of what is just wrote is not true.

There is a girl in my grade who most of the time is getting made fun of or embarrassing herself because she is trying too hard to impress everybody. It's either she's not smart enough, or she's not skinny enough or she's not athletic and for several other reasons. Nothing she does is ever enough for anyone.

Almost everybody makes fun of this girl. It is not just certain people. Even I have made fun of her before. I really regret it now though. Nobody should have to put up with what she puts up with every day.

One time when I was in 7th grade our principal had a meeting in the auditorium to talk to us about the disrespect and bullying we all have towards other students. She told us that she had parents calling her practically crying on the phone because their children were getting bullied in school. She told us that we need to start respecting each other a little bit more. After that a little bit of it stopped, but not much. It just didn't sink in to most of us that we were hurting people's feeling and that it wasn't just harmless fun. I knew she was mostly talking about this girl, but she never said any actual names.

This girl is not the only one that gets bullied in our school. Tons of kids self-esteem gets lowered every day because some jerk who decides to make fun of them or pick on them. I think maybe kids should start sticking up for each other more. That is the problem with our schools, not enough kids have the courage to stick up for others. They all just follow and laugh with everybody else.

There have been so many school shootings because of kids who decide to make fun of or neglect other kids. I definitely don't want to be the one that pushes another kid to bring a gun to school.

LETTER #5

It all started in the second grade. Our teacher was Mr. Waltney, the funnest and funniest teacher ever. Back then everyone had fun. Whenever we went to recess, there was always someone else to jump with, or hopscotch with, or play kickball with.

Everybody had someone else. Except Mickey. It was as if Mickey didn't have a last name. Nobody knew it. Nobody used it. To the students, Mickey's full name was just Mickey. One time his pants fell down in kickball. People poked him and called names every day, including me. We'd do it enough until he'd cry and then we'd keep doing it and calling him a cry-baby. But Mickey never told anyone, a teacher or counselor or principal. That's why we kept doing it. It was like a new game.

Whenever we teased Mickey, we used physical abuse, like poking or pinching. Back in second grade, it never occurred to me or anyone that this could be really hurtful to Mickey or that it could leave a scar on his self-confidence. Nobody cared what happened to Mickey.

One day, he moved. Nobody knew where or even cared. If anybody missed him it was because they couldn't tease him anymore.

LETTER #6

The day began in first hour in 6th grade. A girl was always sitting there brushing her hair, doing her makeup, painting her nails. She was always doing something. The girl wasn't very smart and was happy at times and sad at times. She was mostly sad though.

Why she was always sad was because people would make fun of her constantly. Why she got made fun of was because of the way she dressed, acted, and caused people to think she wasn't pretty. Deep down inside I knew she was beautiful, like a blossom ready to bloom. Other people didn't look at her that way.

When I saw those people make fun of her I wanted to switch places with her. I didn't want her to suffer from constant teasing and humiliation. Why I wanted to do this was because she had been getting so much teasing all her life and I haven't so I wanted to experience what it would be like not to be teased for a moment in her life.

But I knew in reality I couldn't. I was just sitting there frozen in agony. Wishing someone stop it. But no one did. I had to do it myself. So I did. I walked over there and yelled, STOP! Then it was silence. I couldn't believe I just did that.

Ever since I did that I have always stuck up for people. I think since I did that, that one girl had such a big effect on her life. She has always stood tall and never gave up. That girl is one big blessing from God.

Appendix

ASSESSMENT OF LETTER NAME KNOWLEDGE

This is an example of a very simple instrument that can be administered by parents or teachers to assess whether the student can recognize all the letters of the alphabet. You can duplicate this set of letters or make up one of your own. The key is not to have the letters in alphabetical order and to include all twenty-six letters, upper case and lower case. We also suggest that you not put the lower case b and d next to each other nor the p and q.

Have two copies of the letters, one for the student to read from and one for you to mark any errors by putting a "x' through the letter and writing the letter name the student said instead next to it.

Ask the student to please read the letters to you. If the student should ask you whether he or she should read across or down, respond "Any way you want." Then put an arrow in the direction that the student read, across or down. If the student reads down it may indicate that directionality (automatically reading across) has not been firmly established and is another subskill of reading that needs practice.

Any letters that are missed must be retaught, one at a time. The most common problems are confusion of b and d and p and q. Each letter should be retaught until mastered and then the next letter retaught.

ASSESSMENT OF LETTER NAME KNOWLEDGE

O   H   D   U   F   E

A   G   S   T   W   Z

X   L   R   I   N   B

C   Y   P   J   V   Q   M   K

m   h   g   k   w   j

q   v   y   a   z   u

b   l   c   e   n   s

o   d   x   f   i   t   r   p

References

The American Academy of Child & Adolescent Psychiatry. (2008). "Bullying." Retrieved February 7, 2009 from http://www.aacap.org/page.ww?name=Bullying&section=Facts.

American Academy of Pediatrics. (2011). "Social Media and Kids: Some Benefits, Some Worries." Retrieved April 4, 2011 from http://www.aap/advocacy/releases/june09/social media.htm.

American Academy of Pediatrics. (2011). "Talking to Kids and Teens about Social Media and Sexting." Retrieved April 7, 2011 from http://www.aap/advocacy/releases/june09 social media.htm.

American Bar Association, House of Delegates. (2011). Resolution 107A. February 17.

American Medical Association. (2008). "Violence in the Media." *National Advisory Council on Violence and Abuse.*

Bagley, C., and P. Tremblay. (1997). "Suicidal Behavior in Homosexual and Bisexual Males." *American Journal of Public Health.*

Bale, J. (2004). "Parents of Bullies Are Desperate for Help." Retrieved October 26, 2008 from http://www.timesonline.co.uk/tol/news/uk/article39389 2.ece.

Barros, R. M., E. J. Silver, and E. K. Stein. (2009). "School Recess and Group Classroom Behavior." *Pediatrics* 132 (2).

Bonanno, G. A. (2004). "Loss, Trauma, and Human Resilience—Have We Underestimated the Human Capacity to Thrive after Extremely Aversive Events?" *American Psychologist* 59 (1).

Boulden, W. T. (2006). "Youth Leadership, Racism, and Intergroup Dialogue." *Journal of Ethnic & Cultural Diversity in Social Work* 15 (1/2).

Bradshaw, C. P., and T. E. Waasdorp. (2011). "Effective Strategies in Combating Bullying." White House Conference on Bullying Prevention.

Bradshaw, C. P., T. E. Waasdorp, L. M. O'Brennan, and M. Gulemetova. (2011). "Findings from the NEA's Nationwide Study of Bullying." Washington, DC: National Education Association.

Brown, E. (2011). "Study Finds Teen Bullying Is Linked to Social Status." *Baltimore Sun,* February 8.

Carter, S. (1998). *Civility: Manners, Morals, and the Etiquette of Democracy.* New York: HarperCollins.

Centers for Disease Control and Prevention. (2007). *Morbidity & Mortality Report.*

Centers for Disease Control and Prevention. (2010). *Suicide and Self-Inflicted Injury.*

Cohen-Posey, A. (1995). *How to Handle Bullies, Teasers, & Other Meanies.* Highland City, FL: Rainbow Books.

Costello, J. (2004). "Sibling Bullying." *Journal of Child Psychology and Psychiatry* 29.

Covey, S. (1998). *Seven Habits of Highly Effective Teens.* Whitby, ON: Fireside.

Craig, W., and D. Pepler. (1997). "Observations of Bullying and Victimization in the School Yard." *Canadian Journal of School Psychology* 13 (2).

Crary, D. (2009). "Report: Most States Lag with Dating-Violence Laws." Retrieved March 24, 2009 from http://news.yahoo.com/s/ap/20090324/ap_on_us/.

Cullen, D. (2009). *Columbine.* New York: Hachette Book Group.

Dodge, K., and J. Coie. (1987). "Social Information Processing Factors in Reactive and Proactive Aggression in Children's Peer Groups." *Journal of Personality and Social Psychology* 3.

Dubow, F. (2009). Interview on the Columbia County Longitudinal Study. Retrieved January 29, 2009 from http://www.toledoblade.com/apps/pbcs.dll/article?AID=/20061113/.

Elias, M. (2002). "Kids' Meanness Might Mean Health Risks When They Grow Up." *USA Today,* September 26.

Espelage, D. L. (2007). "Bullying in Early Childhood." Retrieved November 18, 2008 from http://illinoisearlylearning.org/askanexpert/eespelage/trans.htm.

Espelage, D., and S. M. Swearer. (2004). *Bullying in American Schools—A Social-Ecological Perspective on Prevention and Intervention.* New Jersey: Lawrence Erlbaum Associates, Inc.

Finkelhor, D., H. Turner, and R. Ormrod. (2006). "Kid's Stuff: The Nature and Impact of Peer and Sibling Violence on Younger and Older Children." *Child Abuse & Neglect* 30 (12).

Fried, S., and P. Fried. (1996). *Bullies & Victims—Helping Your Child through the Schoolyard Battlefield.* New York: M. Evans and Company.

Fried, S., and P. Fried. (2003). *Bullies, Targets, & Witnesses—Helping Children Break the Pain Chain.* New York: M. Evans and Company.

Galinsky, E., and K. Salmond. (2002). "Youth and Violence: Students Speak Out for a More Civil Society." *Families and Work Institute.*

Garbarino, J. (2006). *See Jane Hit: Why Girls Are Growing More Violent and What We Can Do about It.* New York: Penguin.

Gilligan, C. (1982). *In a Different Voice.* Cambridge: Harvard University Press.

Gladwell, M. (2002). *The Tipping Point: How Little Things Can Make a Big Difference.* New York: Back Bay Books.

Gossen, D. (2008). *It's All about WE—Rethinking Discipline Using Restitution.* Saskatoon, SK: Canada Chelsom Consultants Limited.

Haber, J., with J. Glatzer. (2007). *Bullyproof Your Child for Life.* New York: Pedigree Books.

Haber, J. D., and S. B. Haber. (2007). "Cyberbullying: A 'Virtual' Camp

Nightmare?"*Camping Magazine*. May/June.

Harris, J. R. (1999). *The Nurture Assumption*. New York: Touchstone Books.

High, B., ed. (2007). *Bullycide in America—Moms Speak Out about the Bullying/Suicide Connection*. Darlington, MD: JBS Publishing.

Hillman, C. B. (1995). *Before the School Bell Rings*. Portsmouth, NH: Heinemann.

Hinduja, S., J. W. Patchin. (2011). "Overview of Cyberbullying." White House Conference on Bullying Prevention. March 10.

Hoffman, J. (2010). "As Bullies Go Digital, Parents Play Catch-Up." *New York Times*, December 5.

Horne, R. H., and G. Sugai. (2005). "School-wide Positive Behavior Support: Analternative Approach to Discipline in Schools." *Positive Behavior Support*. New York: Guilford Press.

Huebner, A. (2002). "Adolescent Bullying. Virginia Cooperative Extension." Publication Number 350852. Retrieved February 7, 2009 from http://www.ext.vt.edu/pubs/family/350-852/350-852.html.

Husemann, L. R., L. Eron, M. M. Lefkowitz, and L. O. Walder. (1984). "Stability of Aggression Over Time and Generations." *Developmental Psychology* 20 (6).

Huston, A., and M. Ripke. eds. (2006). *Development Contexts in Middle Childhood*. Cambridge, UK: Cambridge University Press.

Ingersoll, R. M. (2002). "High Turnover Plagues Schools." *USA Today*, August 15.

Johnson, J., P. Cohen, F. Smailes, S. Kasen, and J. Brook. (2002). "Television Viewing and Aggressive Behavior During Adolescence and Adulthood." *Science* 295 (5564).

Jordan, W.J., J. Lara, and J. M. McPartland. (1996). "Exploring the Causes of Early Dropout among Race, Ethnic, and Gender Groups." *Youth and Society* 28 (1).

Kowalski, R. M., S. P. Limber, and P. W. Agatson. (2007). *Cyberbullying: Bullying in the Digital Age*. Oxford, UK: Blackwell.

Laidman, J. (2006). "Is Age 8 Too Late? Kids Who Don't Play Well with Others May Not Be Successful Adults." *Toledo Blade*. Retrieved January 29, 2009 from http://toledoblade.com/apps/pbcs/dll/article?AID=/20061113/.

Landry, D. (2008). "The Utilization of Creative Expression as a Means for Bullying Prevention While Creating a Respectful Environment." Paper delivered at 5th Annual Conference of the International Bullying Prevention Association, Indianapolis, IN. November 6 and 7.

McCaffety, E. (2006). "Bullies Online and in Chat Rooms." National Teen Dating Abuse Helpline. Retrieved November 18, 2008 from loveisrespect.org.

Mendel, D. (2010). Annie E. Casey Report on the Missouri Division of Youth Services. Retrieved from http//www.missouriapproach.org/publications/2010/12/8/annie-e-casey-foundation-report.html.

Menninger, K. A. (1971). *The Human Mind*. 3rd ed. New York: Alfred A. Knopf.

Montessori School of Tokyo. (2009). "Sunshine: Goals." Retrieved January 1/26, 2009 from http://montessorijapan.com/Index,php/sp-goals.

Mysilk, L. (2008). "Connect with Kids: Weekly News Stories: Grade School Bullying." Retrieved November 13, 2008 from http://www.connectwithkids.com/tipsheet/2008/394_jul 16/thisweek.

Nansel, T. R., M. Overpeck, R. Pilla, W. J. Ruan, B. Simons-Morton, and P. Scheidt. (2001). "Bullying Behaviors among U.S. Youth: Prevalence and Association with

Psychosocial Adjustment." *Journal of the American Medical Association* 285 (16).

NEA Health Information Network. (2005). Statistics: "Gun Violence in Our Communities." Retrieved July 14, 2008 from http://www.neahin.org/programs/schoolsafety/gunsafety/statistics.htm.

Nickelodeon and the Kaiser Family Fund. (2000–2001). "Talking with Kids." National Survey of Parents and Kids, conducted between December 9, 2000 and January 18, 2001.

Olweus, D. (1993). *Bullying at School—What We Know and What We Can Do.* Oxford, UK: Blackwell.

Organization for Economic Cooperation and Development. (2008). "Education at a Glance 2008." OECD Indicators. Indicator A1 and A2. Paris: OECD Publications. Retrieved from http://www.oecd.org/document/9/0,3343,en2649392632384126676111111,00.html.

Parker-Pope, T. (2009). "What Are Friends For—A Longer Life." *New York Times,* April 20.

Parker-Pope, T. (2011). "Web of Popularity, Achieved by Bullying." *New York Times,* February 15.

Peterson, J., and K. E. Ray. (2006). "Bullying among the Gifted: The Subjective Experience." *Gifted Child Quarterly* 50 (3).

Public Agenda. (1999). "Kids These Days '99: What Americans Really Think about the Next Generation." New York: Public Agenda.

Richmond, R. (2010). "Some Ways to Thwart an Online Bully." *New York Times,* August 18.

Riley, P. (2004). "Five Years after Columbine: Students Take the Lead to Stop School Violence." Raleigh, NC: *National Association of S.A.V.E.*

Roche, T. (2001). "Voices from the Cell." *Time* 157 (21). May 28.

Sager, N. W., and C. Garrity. (2008). "Bully Prevention in Early Childhood Education: Collaboration Between Teachers and Families. Retrieved October 16, 2008 from www.article_print http://www.earlychildhoodnews./earlychildhood/article_print.aspx?ArticleID=736.

Selman, R., and A. Demorest. (1984). "Observing Troubled Children's Interpersonal Negotiation Strategies: Implications of and for a Developmental Model." *Child Development* 55 (1).

Shore, K. (2005). *The ABC's of Bullying Prevention.* New York: Dude Publishing.

Shriver, T., and R. P. Weissberg. (2005). "No Emotion Left Behind." *New York Times,* August 16.

Stern, J. (2009). *Parenting Is a Contact Sport: 8 Ways to Stay Connected to Your Kids for Life.* Austin, TX: Greenleaf Book Group Press.

Toppo, G. (2009). "Profound Shift in Home Schooling." *USA Today,* May 29–31.

Turgade, M., and B. L. Fredrickson. (2004). "Resilient Individuals Use Positive Emotions to Bounce Back from Negative Emotional Experiences." *Journal of Personality and Social Psychology* 86 (2).

U.S. Department of Education. (2005–2006). Common Core of Data.

Vossekuil, B., R. Fein, M. Reddy, R. Borum, and W. Modzeleski. (2004). The Final Report of the Safe School Initiative. U.S. Department of Education/U.S. Secret Service.

Wepman, J. M., and W. M. Reynolds. (1987). Wepman's Auditory Discrimination Test (ADT), 2nd ed. Los Angeles: Western Psychological Services.

Wheelock,W., N. Silvaroli, and C. Campbell. (2008). *The Classroom Reading Inventory*. 11th ed. New York: McGraw Hill.

Wiehe, V. R. (1997). *Sibling Abuse—What Parents Need to Know About*. Springville, UT: Bonneville Books.

Wilborn, D. (2008). "Adolescent Bullying." Retrieved January 30, 2009 from http://www.accessnorthga.com/detail.php?n=209766.

Wilson, J. (1995). *The Moral Sense*. New York: Free Press.

World Health Organization. (1989). World Health Statistics.

Index

Abbott, Jim, 69
abuse: adolescent dating, 66–67; child, vii, 1, 11, 16–17, 24; defined, 11, 24; peer, vii, 1, 11
ACA. *See* American Camp Association
academic performance, 12–13
accomplices, 33
achievement, 13, 73, 96, 136, 140, 155
Adams, Rebecca G., 148
ADD. *See* attention deficit disorder
Adderall XR, 70
ADHD. *See* attention deficit hyperactivity disorder
administrators, 8, 93–97, 106, 135
adolescent dating abuse, 66–67
adolescents. *See* high-school bullying
adults: as mentors, 155; student engagement with support from, 107–10
affiliation, 136, 148
Afteb, Parry, 44
aggression, relational, 136
aggressive responses, 146
aliases, 45
alternative schooling, 141
American Academy of Child and Adolescent Psychiatry, 64

American Academy of Pediatrics, 47, 154
American Bar Association, 18
American Camp Association (ACA), 51–52, 54
American Civil Liberties Union, 46
American Girl dolls, 89
American Journal of Public Health, 14
American Medical Association, 15, 28
anger, 1–3, 28–29, 155. *See also* rage
Animal Farm, 72
Annie's story, 72–73
anonymity, as cyberbullying, 45
anonymous tip boxes, 110
antibullying, 99, 157–58; legislation, 15, 43–44, 46, 102, 112–13, 157–58; parent sessions on, 46, 102
Antonopoulos, Pat, 78–79
apologies, 7–8, 85, 99, 127–29
arts: classes, 109; value of, 97
art teachers, 105–6
Asperger, Hans, 28
Asperger's syndrome, 27–28, 31
assertive responses, 146
athletics, 96
at-risk students, 76
attention deficit disorder (ADD), 27, 69–71

attention deficit hyperactivity disorder (ADHD), 27, 31, 69–71, 78, 129
authoritarian parents, 152
autism, 27–28, 69

Barbie Brats, 63
Barros, Romina M., 95
Barrow, Bryan, 26–27
Bashaw, Betty Barker, x
bedwetting, 75–76
Before the School Bell Rings (Hillman), 59
belief, 5
Bell, Alexander Graham, 69
Bennet, Judy, 101
Berkley, Bert, 91
betrayal, 38
Blackhawk Middle School, 88
Blitt, Rita, x, 90
blockers, 33
Blue Valley School District, 90
body language, 146
books, 14–15, 105, 136
bossiness, 59–60
Boston Globe, 155
Bowling Green State University, 62
boy bulliers, 36, 126–27
Boy Scouts, 156
Branson, Missouri, 111–12
Bratton, William, 83
Braun, Don, 152
Broken Windows theory, 83
Brooks Elementary School, 106
Brown, Steven, 46
buddies, for new students, 102
"Bullied to Death" investigative report, 129–30
bulliers, 2, 21–22, 96; boy, 36, 126–27; defined, 25; elitist, 29–30; girl, 36, 40, 102, 126–27, 136–37, 140–41, 148; with high status parents, 142; letters about, 161–65; parents' checklist, 153; parents of, 99, 133–34, 142, 150–53; profiles of, 29–30; punishments for, 46, 105, 108, 140–42; in SES example, 123–26; teacher colleagues as, 135–36; teachers helping, 137–38; teen, 65

Bullies, Targets & Witnesses—Helping Children Break the Pain Chain (Fried and Fried), viii, 25, 129, 154
"Bullies Go Digital, Parents Play Catch-up" (Hoffman), 47
Bullies & Victims—Helping Your Child Through the Schoolyard Battlefield (Fried and Fried), 9, 25
bullycide, 14–15, 123
Bullycide in America—Moms Speak Out about the Bullying/Suicide Connection, 14–15
bully-free classrooms, 60–61, 134
bully-free summer camps, 39, 51–57
bullying: awareness of, v–vii; defining, 21–22, 24; dimensions and overview of, 9–19; dynamics of, 1–8, 2–4; early childhood, 59–61; electronic, 156; emotional, 35–36, 38–40, 121–22, 126, 147–49, 162; extent of, 22; high school, 65–66; kindness replacing, 89–91; legal aspects, 17; letters about, 161–65; middle school, 64; nonverbal emotional, 38–39; origins, 27–34; peer, 19; peer abuse, vii, 1, 11; physical, 35–37, 39–40, 121–22, 126, 145–47; psychological emotional, 38–39; sexual, 35–36, 39–41, 64, 121–22, 126, 149; sibling, 8, 18–19, 27, 74, 153; as societal concern, 22–24; of special needs students, viii, 69–79, 162; teasing *vs.*, 24; as term, avoiding use of, 133–34, 138; terminology, 24–26; trends in, 35–36; verbal, 35, 37–38, 40–41, 121–22, 126, 145–47, 162; verbal sexual, 40–41. *See also* antibullying; cyberbullying; prevention
"Bullying Behaviors Among U.S. Youth: Prevalence and Association with Psychosocial Adjustment," 22
BullyPolice, 112
Bully Police USA, 22, 158
Bullyproof Your Child or Life (Haber, J., and Glatzer, J.), 48
BullySafeUSA, 89, 117, 130–31, 135

Burke, Chris, 69
bus drivers, 103–5
bystander, 26

cafeterias, 95
cafeteria workers, 103–5
California Association of Private School
    Organizations (CAPSO), 133
camp counselors, 55–56
camper training, 54–55
Campfire, 156
camps. *See* summer camps
CAPSO. *See* California Association of
    Private School Organizations
Caring Community Sites, 92
carpool rules, 157
Catawba County Medical Society
    Alliance, 33
CDC. *See* Centers for Disease Control
    and Prevention
Celebration of Good Behavior, 87
Center for Health Communication,
    Harvard School of Public Health, 88
Centers, Learning, 78–79
Centers for Disease Control and
    Prevention (CDC), 14
champions, 33, 110
change, of culture, viii, x, 1–8;
    challenge of, 81–92; PBIS, 87–88;
    peer and community influence,
    86–87; saturation effect, 88
Change Agents, viii, 158; art teachers,
    105–6; bus drivers, 103–5; cafeteria
    workers, 103–5; classroom teachers,
    98–100; community, 110–12;
    custodians, 103–5; multimedia
    center specialists, 105; music
    teachers, 105–6; national, 113–14;
    para-professionals, 101; physical
    education instructors, 100;
    playground supervisors, 106; policy
    makers, 112–14; school counselors,
    psychologists, and social workers,
    101–3; school crossing guards, 107;
    school nurses, 100, 103; school
    principal/administrators, 93–97;
    secretaries, 106–7; special education

teachers, 100–101; SROs, 107;
    student engagement with adult
    support, 107–10; vice-principals,
    97–98. *See also* parents
character education, 95, 111
Character Plus Conference, 111
*The Checklist Manifesto: How to Get
    Things Right* (Gawande), 47
child abuse, vii, 1, 11, 16–17, 24
child pornography, 17–18
Children and Adults with Attention-
    Deficit/Hyperactivity Disorder, 71
children's literature, 136
Cho, Seung-Hui, 3–4
Churchill, Winston, 69
Circle of Friends, 101
Civil Rights Act, of 1964, 149
classrooms: bully free, 60–61;
    discussions about prevention,
    101–2, 142–43; teachers as Change
    Agents, 98–100
cliques, 53, 84, 127, 136–37, 148
Code of Conduct, 94, 97, 103, 110,
    134, 142, 157
Cohen-Posey, Alice, 146
Coie, John, 29
Cole, Mary Jane, 89–90
colleagues, as bulliers, 135–36
College of the Ozarks, 111
Collegial Coaches, 135
Columbia County Longitudinal Study,
    62
Columbia University, 155
Columbine (Cullen), 23
Columbine High School, 23
Committee for Children, 18
Commonsense Media, 29
community, 86–87, 110–12
community service, 96
complying, 31
computer use, 149, 156
Concerta, 70
context. *See* Power of Context
Conversation Bench, 106
counselors: camp, 55–56; school, 100–
    103, 117–19, 148–49
courage, 27, 41, 127–29, 137, 139, 164

courtesy, 158
Covey, Stephen, 85
Craig, Wendy, 26
crime, 16–18, 124
crossing guards, 107
Cruise, Tom, 69
Cry, Comply, Deny, Fly-Off-the-Handle
    syndrome, 31
crying, 31
Cullen, Dave, 23
culture, changing, viii, x, 1–8; challenge
    of, 81–92; PBIS, 87–88; peer and
    community influence, 86–87;
    saturation effect, 88. *See also* Change
    Agents
Currie, Nikki, 79
custodians, 103–5
cutting, 36
cyberbullying, 35, 113, 121–23, 126;
    checklist, 48–49; defined, 42–44;
    early start of, 63–64; parents and,
    46–49, 149–51; responsibility for
    responding to, 44; solutions, 46–49;
    Task Force on, 109–10; types, 45–46.
    See also sexting
cyber stalking, 45

Darling-Hammond, Linda, 75
Davis, Joan, 111
Davis, Richard, 147
Dawes, William, 82
Dean, Dorothy, 39
Decker, Tim, 142
defense strategies, 27
DeJesus, Jacque, 90
denigration, 45
Denny, Rhonda, 126
denying, 31
Department of Education, U.S., 113
depression, 3, 136
*Development Contexts in Middle
    Childhood* (Huston and Ripke), 62
discipline, 96, 140–42
Disney, Walt, 69
dissing, 111
Division of Family Services, Missouri,
    91

documentation, 150
Dodge, Kenneth, 29
Dombo, Julie, 84
drama classes, 109
driving habits, 88–89, 155
drop-out problems, 11–12
Dubow, Eric F., 62–63
Duke, Patty, 69
Duncan, Arne, 91, 113
Durlak, Joseph, 96
DVDs/videos, 130, 143
dyslexia, 69

early childhood: bullying, 59–61;
    Learning Centers for, 78–79
early intervention, 60, 62–63
Edison, Thomas, 69
Education Amendment Act, of 1972, 17
Edwin Green Elementary School, 94
electronic bullying, 156
ELF. *See* Emotional Learning
    Foundation
Eliot, Charles, 51
elitist bulliers, 29–30
emotional bullying, 35, 38–40, 121–
    22, 126, 147–49, 162
Emotional Learning Foundation (ELF),
    89
empathizers, 33
empathy, 7, 60, 98–100, 106, 127, 129
empowerment, 8, 87, 146. *See also*
    Student Empowerment Session
enabling, 153
epidemic, 81–83
Eron, Leonard, 16, 62, 124
Espelage, Dorothy, 25, 59
etiquette, 155, 158
exclusion, 38, 45

Facebook, 48, 149, 151
family issues, 27
Fechter, Debbie, 106
female gossiping, 148
Finkelhor, David, 18
Finland, 75–76
Fischer, Mary, 135
flaming, 45

flying off the handle, 31
Formspring, 48, 149
Forrest Elementary School, 95
free-lunch programs, 104
free-speech rights, 46
Fried, Paula, 9, 21, 25, 120–21, 129, 154
Fried, SuEllen, vi–vii, x–xi, 1, 5, 9, 11, 13, 15, 19, 21, 25–26, 33, 38, 84, 89–90, 113, 117, 129–30, 133, 136, 154
friendships, 148

Gandhi, Mohandas, 7, 93
Garbarino, James, x, 148
Garvin-Richardson, Kimberly, 95
Gawande, Atul, 47
gender discrimination, 40
gender orientation, 96, 113
George, Alyssa, 11
Gifted Child Quarterly, 78
gifted students, 76–80
Gilligan, Carol, 136
girl bulliers, 36, 40, 102, 126–27, 136–37, 140–41, 148
Girl Scouts, 137, 156
Giuliani, Rudolph, 83
giving, value of. *See* volunteerism
Gladwell, Malcolm, x, 81–86. *See also* change, of culture; Power of Context
Glatzer, Jenna, 48
Goldberg, Carey, 155
Gossen, Diane, 108
gossip, 38, 148
Grand Theft Auto, 28
Guardino, Brandi, 32–33
Gunn, Frederick, 51
Gunnery Camp, 51

Haber, Joel, 43, 48
Haber, Scott B., 49
Hackett, Phil, 94
harassment, 40, 45. *See also* sexual harassment
Harris, Eric, 23
Harris, Judith, 86
Harvard School of Public Health, 88

Harvard University, 51, 88, 148
Head, Sue, 111–12
health issues, 15–16, 103
Healthy Families America, 154
high-school bullying, 65–66
Hillman, Carol B., 59–60
Hoffman, Ian, 47
home schooling, 90, 140
Home Visitor, 154
homosexuality, 14, 17, 39, 41, 113, 122, 139
hot spots, 53–54, 95
Howard County school system, 17
How to Handle Bullies, Teasers and Other Meanies (Cohen-Posey), 146
The Human Mind (Menninger), 125
humor, 98, 147
Hurricane Katrina, 158
Huston, Aletha, 62

impersonation, 45
inborn traits, 27–28, 70
Informal Reading Inventory, 73
Ingersoll, Richard M., 14
intentional pain, 4
Internet, 49–50, 63–64. *See also* cyberbullying
isolation, 39
It's All About WE, Rethinking Discipline Using Restitution (Gossen), 108

jealousy, 13, 66, 79
Johnston, Debby, x, 15
judgers, 33
Juvenile Justice Center, 73–74
juvenile justice system, 17, 141–42

Kanner, Leo, 28
Kansas prison program, 110–11
karate, 71
Keeter Center for Character Education, 111
Kelling, George, 83
Kim's Story, 84, 120–21
Kindest Kansas Citizen, 90
kindness, bullying replaced by, 89–91
Kindness Activities Program, 90

Kindness Rap, 158
Kindness Song, 106, 114–15
King, Martin Luther, Jr., 7
Klebold, Dylan, 23
Kurtis, Bill, 129

Ladd, Gary, 30
Laidman, Jenni, 63
Lampitt, Pam, 18
Lang, Lynne, 19, 25, 89, 130
Law of the Few, 84, 110
Learning Centers, 78–79
learning disabilities. *See* special needs
    students
learning issues, 12–13
legislation, antibullying, 15, 43–44, 46,
    103, 112–13, 157–58
Letter Name Knowledge assessment, 74
letters, from children, 161–65
Levanthal, Howard, 83
life-skill training, 96
LINC. *See* Local Investment
    Commission
Liz Clairborne, Inc., 66
Local Investment Commission (LINC),
    91
locker rooms, 105
Logan, Jessica, 41
loveisrespect.org, 66

MADD. *See* Mothers Against Drunk
    Driving
manners, 158
Mariner Middle School, 85–86, 93–94
The Marshmallow Test, 155
martial arts, 71, 147
Matlin, Marlee, 69
Matthews, Karen, 15
McFadden, Tom, 98
Mean Girls (film), 136
media: anger and images in, 28–29;
    antibullying legislature and, 15;
    influence, 28–29; social, vii, 47–48,
    149. *See also* cyberbullying
medications, 70–71, 103
Mendel, Dick, 142
Menninger, Karl, 125

Menninger, Rosemary, 12
mentors, 102, 108, 135, 155
metal detectors, in schools, 37
middle childhood, 62–63
middle school: bullying, 64; SES
    experiences at, 129
Mischel, Walter, 155
Missouri Division of Youth Services,
    141–42
Missouri Learning Disabilities
    Association, 71
Mix-It-Up at Lunch Day, 109
Montessori School, 61, 64
The Moral Sense (Wilson), 108
Mothers Against Drunk Driving
    (MADD), 88–89
motor control, 76–77
multimedia center specialist, 105
Multiple Intelligences Inventory, 74
music teachers, 105–6
Mysilk, Louise, 63
MySpace, 48, 151

National Attention Deficit Disorder
    Association, 71
National Center for Social Norming,
    143
National Crime Prevention Council,
    149
National Education Association, 11
National Pre-kindergarten Study (NPS),
    141
National Teen Dating Abuse Helpline,
    66
National Youth Violence Prevention
    Resource Center, 11
Natural Helpers program, 84, 108
Netherlands, 75
New York City Police Department, 83
New York Times, 13, 47, 148
No Child Left Behind Act, 13
nonverbal emotional bullying, 38–39
No Put-Down Zone, 157
Norway, 75
NPS. *See* National Pre-kindergarten
    Study
nurses, 100, 103

The Nurture Assumption (Harris, J.), 86

Obama, Barack, 91, 113
Odd Girl Out (Simmons), 136
O'Keefe, Gwenn, 47
Olweus, Dan, 17
Open Door policy, 96
Operation Smile, 89
Ophelia Project, 137
outing, 45

pain: anger intensity and, 1;
    intentional, 4; rage, and revenge
    cycle, 1–4, *2–4*, 123; used to societal
    advantage, 6–7; universal, 4–5
Pakula, Sidney, 75
Palacco, Patricia, 69
panels, 109
para-professionals, 101
The Parent Educator, 154
Parenting is a Contact Sport (Stern),
    158–59
Parentline Plus, 152
parents: as advocates, vi, 76, 156–59;
    antibullying sessions for, 46, 102;
    authoritarian, 152; bullier checklist
    for, 153; of bulliers, 99, 133–34,
    142, 150–53; camp checklist for, 56;
    cyberbullying and, 46–49, 149–51;
    high status, with bully children, 142;
    important themes for, xii; meeting
    on bullying prevention, 158–59;
    as partners, 154–56; as protectors,
    145–54; as role models, 19, 133,
    154, 156–57; schools contacted by,
    150–51; seminars for, 46, 150; of
    targets, 134, 145–51; of witnesses,
    153–54
Parents As Teachers, 154
Parker-Pope, Tara, 148
Park Ridge-Niles School District, 89
Partners Linking Arms for Character
    Education (PLACE), 111–12
passive responses, 146
passive targets, 31
PBIS. *See* Positive Behavior
    Interventions and Support

Peace Table, 61, 64
peer abuse, vii, 1, 11
peer bullying, related to sibling
    bullying, 19
peer influence, 86
peer mentoring, 102, 108
Pepler, Debra, 26
Peterson, Jean Sunde, 78–79
physical bullying, 35–37, 39–40, 121–
    22, 126, 145–47
physical education instructors, 100,
    136–37
PLACE. *See* Partners Linking Arms for
    Character Education
playgrounds, 106
playground supervisors, 106
policy makers, 112–14
Polsky, Norman, x, 90
Poplau, Ron, 109
Positive Behavior Interventions and
    Support (PBIS), 87–88
Potts, Jason, 13
power, detrimental, vii, 19
Power of Context, 82–83, 85–87
"Power of Kindness," 90
pre-camp professional development, 54
prevention, 7, 105, 107; classroom
    discussions about, 101–2, 142–43;
    importance of, 22, 60; parent
    meeting on, 158–59; programs and
    plans, 97–99, 131, 140; staff training
    on, 135; White House Conference
    on, 86–87, 113
principals, 8, 93–97, 106, 135, 139–40
prisons, 5–6, 39, 110–11
proactive bulliers, 29
professional ethics, 135
Proponents for Creative Expression
    programs, 97
provocative targets, 31
Pryor, Fred, 91
pseudonyms, 45
psychological emotional bullying,
    38–39
Psychological Science, 155
psychologists, 101–3
PTA/PTO, 46, 87, 97, 105–6, 158

pull factors, 11–12
punishments, 46, 105, 108, 140–42
Purdue University, 78
push factors, 11

Queen Bees and Wannabees (Wiseman), 136
Queen's University, 26

RA. *See* relational aggression
rage, 1–4, *2–4*, 123, 155
rape, 17
Reaching Out From Within prison program, 5–6, 111–12
reactive bulliers, 29
reading skills, 71–74, 155
reason, belief trumping, 5
recess, 106, 121
relational aggression (RA), 136
reporting, 54, 99, 138, 143, 153
resilience, 155–56
resources, 24, 48, 54, 75, 102, 105, 135
respect, 147, 155
responsibilities, 155–56
restitution, 108
restorative justice, 108
retaliation, 2, 19, 22, 31, 143
retribution, 2
revenge, 1–4, *2–4*, 6, 123
Revere, Paul, 82
Reynolds, Dave, 139
ridicule, 2, 96, 99, 118, 153
Ripke, Marika, 62
Ritalin, 70
Robinson, Nicole, 88
Roche, Timothy, 6
Rockefeller, Nelson, 69
role models, 19, 133, 154, 156–57
role-playing, 146
Roosevelt Elementary School, 89
Rouse, Stephen, 101
rudeness, 157
rumors, 38
Rutgers, 40

Santana High School, 6
saturation effect, 88–89

Saucier, Kathleen, ix, 85, 94
Save Our Kids, 33
scapegoating, 32
Scarsdale Middle School, 147
school resource officers (SRO), 48, 107
schools: administrators, 8, 93–97, 106, 135; alternative, 141; counselors, 100–103, 117–19, 148–49; crossing guards, 107; metal detectors in, 37; nurses, 100, 103; parents contacting, 150–51; positive environment at, 61–62; principals, 8, 93–97, 107, 135, 139–40; psychologists, 101–3; responsibilities of, 156; shootings at, 1, 3–4, 6, 9–10, 23, 65, 122; weapons in, 10, 36–37
Scott, January, 67
Scruggs, J. Daniel, 79
Sebelius, Kathleen, 113
secretaries, 106–7
secret betrayal, 38
Secret Service, U.S., 6
See Jane Hit (Garbarino), 148
self-mutilation, 36
self-protectors, 33
Selman, Robert, 29
SES. *See* Student Empowerment Session
Seven Habits of Highly Effective Teens (Covey), 85
sex offenders, history of, 41
sexting (sex-texting), 17–18, 41
sexual bullying, 35, 39–41, 64, 121–22, 126, 149
sexual harassment, 40, 149
sexual language, 96, 113, 122, 139, 163
Shawnee Mission, KS School District, 89, 101, 109
shootings, at schools, 1, 3–4, 6, 9–10, 23, 65, 122
Shriver, Timothy, 13
siblings: bullying, 8, 18–19, 27, 74, 153; comparing, 99
sleepover rules, 157
Smith, Ruth, 155
smoking, 82–83
snitches, 26, 125, 138
social epidemic, 81–83

social media, vii, 47–48, 149
social skills, 60–61, 155–56
social workers, 101–3
Socratic method, of asking questions, 118
Sosland, Blanche, vi, ix, xi, 11, 55, 73–75, 90
Southern Poverty Law Center, 89, 109
special education teachers, 78–79, 100–101
special needs students: Annie's story, 72–73; bullying of, viii, 69–79, 162; diagnosis of, 69, 71–79; evaluation tools, 73; gifted, 76–80; individualized attention for, 75–76; Informal Reading Inventory, 73; Letter Name Knowledge assessment, 74; medication debate, 70–71; parent advocacy, 76; teachers of, 78–79, 100–101; three-step process for, 72; twice-exceptional, 76–78; Wepman Test of Auditory Discrimination, 74–75
sports, 96, 157
sports stars, 96, 102
SRO. *See* school resource officers
staff training, 56, 93, 130, 135
Stanford University, 75, 98
Stangler, Gary, 91
Stephen F. Austin State University, 117, 131
Stephen Mack Middle School, 105
Stern, Joanne, 158–59
Stickiness Factor, 82–85, 129
Stop Teasing Me! (video), 119
storytelling, 147
Strauss, Murray, 18
Student Empowerment Session (SES), 84–85, 88, 101, 108, 135, 140; advance preparation, 118–19; example of, 120–29; overview, 117–18; tips on, 129–30
students: at-risk, 76; empowerment of, 8, 87, 146; engagement with adult support, 107–10; new, buddies for, 102; role of, vi, 33–34; witness training for, 96, 108, 139. *See also* special needs students

suicide, 3, 6, 14–15, 33, 41, 123
summer camps, 39, 51–57
Sweden, 75
Sweeney, Elizabeth, 152

talking rocks, 106
talking tree, 106
"Talking With Kids About Tough Issues," 11
targets, 21–22, 105, 131, 138; defined, 25; parents of, 134, 145–51; profiles of, 30–31; in SES example, 123–26
Task Force on Cyberbullying, 109–10
Tassoni, John, 46
tattling, 26, 54, 125, 138, 153
teachers: art, 105–6; as bulliers, 135–36; bulliers helped by, 137–38; as Change Agents, 98–101, 105–6; classroom, 98–100; handling parents of bulliers, 142; music, 105–6; parents partnering with, 156; shortages of, 14; of special needs students, 78–79, 100–101; support for, vii, 14, 75–76, 140; tenured, 135; witnesses and, 26–27, 124, 135
Teaching Tolerance magazine, 89, 109
tears, 147
teasing, *vs.* bullying, 24
technology skills, 49–50
teen bulliers, 65
television, 28–29, 154
tenured teachers, 135
Terranova, Andrew, 117, 131
Thirkell, Scott, 107
"30 Activities for Getting Better at Getting Along" (Fried, S., and Lang, L.), 89, 130
three-step process, for special needs students, 72
Tillman Elementary School, 106
Time magazine, 6
The Tipping Point (Gladwell), x, 81–86
Title IX, 17, 149
Title VII, 149
"tool boxes," 79
Train the Trainer Institute, x, 89
trash talk, 38

The Trevor Project, 139
trickery, 45
truancy, 11–12
trust, 128, 139, 149
truth, 26, 38, 124
twice-exceptional students, 76–78. *See also* attention deficit hyperactivity disorder

uniforms, 95
universal pain, 4–5
University of Illinois, at Urbana-Champaign, 25
University of Michigan, 62
University of New Hampshire, 18
University of North Carolina, 148
University of Oregon, 87
University of Pennsylvania, 14
University of Pittsburgh, 15
University Reading Clinic, 74
University Reading Education Department, 72
USA Today, 140

verbal bullying, 35, 37–38, 40–41, 121–22, 126, 145–47, 162
verbal sexual bullying, 40–41
vice-principals, 97–98, 106
victim, 25
video games, 28–29
violence, in media, 28–29
Violence Related Incidents (VRI), 85
Virginia Tech, 3–4
"Voices From The Cell" (*Time* magazine), 6
volunteerism, 96, 102, 108–9, 158
voyeurs, 33

VRI. *See* Violence Related Incidents

Washington, George, 69
weapons, in schools, 10, 36–37
website resources, 48, 54, 135
weight, 13–15
Weisel, Kimberly, 84, 120–21
Weissberg, Roger P., 13, 96
Wepman Test of Auditory Discrimination, 74–75
Werner, Emmy E., 155
"When Push Comes to Shove—Finding Solutions to Bullying Behavior," 67
White House Conference on Bullying Prevention, 86–87, 113
Wiehe, Vernon, 18
Wilborn, Debbie, 65
Williams, Andy, 6
Wilson, James, 83, 108
Wilson, Woodrow, 69
Winsten, Jay, 88–89
WiredKids, 44
WiredSafety, 44
witnesses, vi, 99, 131, 143; defined, 26–27; parents of, 153–54; profiles of, 31–34; in SES example, 123–26; teachers and, 26–27, 124, 135; training for students, 96, 108, 139
word of the month, 111
World Health Organization, 22, 36
writing assignments, 140

Yale University, 83
York University, 26
youth groups, 156
YouTube, 2, 44, 98

About the Authors

SuEllen Fried

SuEllen Fried has spent the past seventeen years interacting with students, K–12, in thirty-six states on bullying issues. Her BullySafeUSA program, featuring the Student Empowerment Session contained in this book, has been introduced to over ninety thousand students. She continues to conduct Train the Trainer Institutes for educators, school counselors, and administrators across the country. She has appeared on the *Today Show*, MSNBC, and was featured in the A&E *Investigative Reports* documentary, "Bullied to Death," narrated by Bill Kurtis. She was a participant in the 2011 White House Conference on Bullying Prevention.

Blanche E. Sosland

Although the major portion of Blanche Sosland's teaching career was at the college and university level, she worked in classrooms ranging from early childhood, Head Start, through middle school. She earned her BA from Barnard College of Columbia University and her MA and PhD from the University of Missouri at Kansas City in Reading Education and Psychology. Her areas of expertise include diagnosis and remediation of reading problems in the classroom and twice exceptional children: gifted and learning disabled. Dr. Sosland is Professor Emerita at Park University in Parkville, Missouri, and an education consultant.